FREE AT LAST

LIVE, LOVE, AND WORK ABROAD: HOW TO FIND JOBS AND BUILD YOUR CAREER ANYWHERE

By

KRISTEN PALANA & JACQUELINE SEIDEL

Copyright © 2017

kpalana.com

oconnell-training.com

eBook Cover Art: *Kristen Palana**

*With awesome cover design feedback and suggestions from members of our Facebook Group, Free At Last: Live, Love & Work Abroad

Special thanks for cover feedback to:

Gidget Harris
Kiersten Pilar Miller
Deborah Wojcicki
Kathleen Fitzsimmons
Matt Sergej Rinc
Vikki Walton
Valerie Chabord
Peggie Bouvier
Anja Pleul
Theresa Garces Johnson

INTRODUCTION

> *"Every dreamer knows that it is entirely possible to be homesick for a place you've never been to, perhaps more homesick than for familiar ground."*
> —— *Judith Thurman*

Have you ever noticed how *smug* some expatriates can be? You know the type. You're minding your own business, checking your email and connecting with friends on Facebook before your workday officially begins.

Boom. There in some annoying sponsored Facebook ad interrupting your friends' posts complaining that it's Monday again, is a smiling, middle-aged couple standing there on some exotic beach locale.

He's wearing a T-shirt and holding a laptop. His tie is thousands of miles away in storage. She's in a sundress with a mini umbrella-clad cocktail in her hand. You can sense she's already had her morning massage.

They stand there gawking at you in your dreary office, hail pelting your window, your inbox up to the wazoo full of boring, mundane invoices and assessment forms. They mock you, big working stiff that you are, with their big smug smiles in front of their ridiculously turquoise beach water and impossibly soft white sand.

The text under their obnoxious photo says something like, "Claim your location-independent lifestyle now" or "Run your business from anywhere in the world" or even "*Nya nya nya nya nyaaaaaaaa!*"

Are you going to take this kind of Monday morning psychological Facebook ad abuse lying down?

This is a book about working your way around the world and making a living even if you don't really live anywhere in particular.

It's about finding ways to finance "working vacations" through short-term jobs when you expect to eventually return home.

It's about finding long-term careers, even soul-affirming life callings abroad when you are not sure you ever want to come back.

Or maybe you want to be your own boss and march to the beat of your own drum either by starting an entrepreneurial enterprise in your newly adopted country or as an all-out *digital nomad* who can never be pinned down to just one place.

This book is about thumbing your nose at the status quo and having international adventures while also being able to put food in your stomach, keep a roof over your head, and pay the bills.

It's about making choices, taking risks, accepting challenges and opportunities, and also about becoming smug yourself. Oh so very smug.

This book is for anyone who would like a taste of expat living no matter your age, gender, goals, or current circumstances.

It's both for people who live to serve and make a difference wherever in the world the wind blows them and also for people who just want to take selfies with their laptop in front of some exotic beach paradise knowing that their bank account will never run empty.

This book is about following your heart while also not losing your head.

So cast off your tie, grab your midday cocktail (optional), and get ready to rumble.

TGIM. "Thank God It's Monday."

Let's explore the possibilities, shall we?

LEGAL NOTES

Finally, nothing in this book is intended to replace common sense, legal, medical, or other professional advice, and is meant to inform, empower, and entertain the reader. So have fun with *Free at Last*, and let's get you started working your way around the world.

TABLE OF CONTENTS

A Bit About Your Smug Authors and How We Can Help You

> *Once you have travelled, the voyage never ends, but is played out over and over again in the quietest of chambers. The mind can never break off from the journey.*
>
> *- Pat Conroy*

KRISTEN (AMERICAN WHO RECENTLY MOVED TO MYANMAR AFTER A DECADE IN ITALY)

Hello and welcome! It's my hope that you'll find the answers you seek about the many working abroad opportunities available to you as a 21st century global citizen.

Our aim in this book is to not only inspire and educate you about the variety of ways to successfully work around the world, but also provide practical advice and solid tips so you can make informed decisions and know what to expect logistically as well as emotionally as a foreigner working abroad.

The first thing I should tell you is that looks can be deceiving. While I may appear smug to those who didn't choose or have the opportunity to live and work abroad, I'm really not much different than anyone else.

Sure, it has been magical being able to sip my morning espresso in a Roman coffee bar, walk through the nearly two thousand year-old arches of the Aurelian Wall that once protected ancient Rome's city center, and help students from all corners of the globe with their digital media projects each day at The American University of Rome for the better part of ten years.

And I love my current existence now as an expatriate living in Yangon, Myanmar helping to set up the new American University of Myanmar, teaching creative professionals at Mango Media, and my semi-part time digital nomad gig as an online professor and writer of e-books.

It all looks amazing on paper and sounds very glamorous but the reality in most places where you might work outside your home country (depending on where that is) is you will need to make sacrifices for the sake of living in your dream destination.

Perhaps you'll only need to make tiny ones that in the end won't matter anyway or perhaps really large ones that can have positive or negative life altering affects moving forward.

Those sacrifices may be that you take a job that pays less than you would make in your home country, you may end up taking jobs that don't require that university degree you just slaved over, or you may struggle daily with linguistic and cultural differences as you strain to learn all the secret handshakes of your new work environment and adopted country.

It could also mean that you make *more* money in your new job than you would at home but struggle with being far away from family and the friends, language, or culture you grew up with.

My own experience includes taking short-term and temporary jobs just after graduating from university back in 1998 in Dublin, Ireland and Edinburgh, Scotland to finance my European travels the year before starting graduate school in New York City.

After returning to the USA for a few years, I've had amazing, life-affirming short-term volunteer work experiences teaching children and adults in India and Tanzania during my summer vacations when I was a graduate student and also a budding educator.

I've also experienced a longer-term overseas career that saw me "graduate" from tenure-track Assistant Professor of Digital Media at William Paterson University in Wayne, New Jersey to a tenured Associate Professor of Digital Media and Program Director of Film and Digital Media at The American University of Rome in Italy. My experience also includes giving short animation and multimedia workshops and presentations abroad in Germany, Singapore, Ethiopia, and now most recently in Myanmar.

I've been known to go rogue a few times as well. In Dublin, Ireland in 1998 I quadrupled my measly waitressing salary by drawing portraits on Grafton Street during my time there (until the weather turned so cold my fingers froze.) I've also moonlighted as a *digital nomad wannabe* while on a leave of absence from my university in Rome, by exploring ways to make a living when you don't live anywhere. For me this has meant teaching online, creating freelance art and design pieces for clients, consulting, and writing e-books.

Finally, as I sit here newly planted in Yangon, Myanmar (formerly called Burma) I have been busy parlaying all of my past work and life experience to help me adapt to the hidden challenges and opportunities of this most recent upheaval.

Somehow after just a few short weeks in Yangon, I moved through total uncertainty and chaos and became a Visiting Professor of Digital Media at the brand new American University of Myanmar while also continuing with my freelance and digital nomad work.

I'd like to share what I've learned these past twenty years or so (Yikes! Has it been that long?) to best help *you* make clear and informed choices about *your* next move.

My fabulous co-author and Australian friend Jacqueline will help you do the same.

Here I'll give you a little backstory. Our friendship began in a rather modern way. We met online in a Facebook group of female online course instructors in late 2014. After commenting on each other's posts with our own goofy senses of humor (and just a few wine and cupcake stickers) we struck up a conversation via private message. Oh yes. We were getting serious!

It turned out that we both up and moved suddenly to new countries in 2006 (Italy for me, Germany for her.) We both had young sons of the same age and we both married (former) East German men. There was a lot to talk about!

Though we learned how much we had in common, I was intrigued by one major difference between us.

I grew up in a small town in southeastern Massachusetts where most people in the 80s did not travel more than 20 miles in any direction. She was a "UN kid," moving countries and continents every few years, wherever the wind blew her family. And yet her son was now growing up like I did, firmly planted in a small, sleepy little town. And my sons are growing up like she did, "UN kids" who spend more time than the average person answering the question, "Where do you come from?"

It wasn't long before I proposed we write a book together, our first one: *Free At Last: Live Love and Work Abroad as a 21st Century Global Citizen.* So Jacqueline then came to Rome to work on it with me last year and we got to finally meet in person. (Oh yes! We had a ball. This time we had real wine and real cupcakes.) And later, before my move to Yangon, I stayed with her in her cozy house in the tiny village of Rentzschmühle, Germany.

So before I hand the mic over to her, one small disclaimer: This is our second book together now and we *still* can't agree on which version of English to use throughout. For this reason, please do excuse that when I write, I use American English and she uses Australian English.

Both versions of English are technically correct though you may notice some slight wording and spelling variations.

In any case, we've found that our words ring more true when we each write using our own styles, so please bear with us and picture us all sitting together at the coffee bar (Jacqui only drinks tea!) as friends and confidants as we help you move forward on your own unique path.

And if you are not quite ready or able yet to take the working abroad plunge any time soon, that's OK as well. Use this book to learn about the possibilities for your own future global adventures. "*Piano piano*" as they say in Italy. Slowly, slowly... there is no rush.

You might also like to check out our first book, _Free At Last: Live Love, and Work Abroad as a 21st Century Global Citizen_ which is a broad introduction and beginner's primer on getting started living a more global lifestyle, be it from the comfort of your own hometown, venturing outside your city or country for the very first time, to longer-term adventures abroad and beyond.

OK Jacqui! Over to you. Can you please explain why you are so smug and how you can help?

JACQUELINE (AUSTRALIAN LIVING IN GERMANY)

Thanks, Kristen!

Apart from our spelling differences, what I really love about working with Kristen and our partnership is how our different backgrounds and experiences shape how we work together and how we can inform and enable you to take that leap outside your comfort zone to work abroad.

I have just celebrated eleven years of living abroad, and while some days it feels like it's been a pretty easy ride, other days I remember the struggles and challenges and the eleven years seem like a hundred. However, in that time I've learned a new profession, learned another language, built a successful business and solid reputation, and helped many businesses and thousands of students improve their communication skills (over 16,000 if I include online students!)

Where in Australia I had the beautiful predictability of my marketing role with the City of Melbourne, regular lunches with colleagues, and walks through Birrarung Marr (or sneaky shopping expeditions on Little Collins Street!), I felt Germany calling and despite the objections of more level-headed people, I heeded the call.

What followed next? Culture shock. A jetlagged airport break-up. Berlin plans made and thrown out the window. Working for a lark and earning peanuts. And somewhere, the growing realisation that actually I was quite good at the lark and it's now something I take very seriously.

Since 2006 I've been building my business and my brand, finding my way through a bureaucracy which sometimes leaves me shaking my head, and a language which sometimes drives me nuts. But I love it. I love this country, this life I've carved out, and most of all that living here enabled me to meet my husband and have our son – the world's youngest astronaut / archaeologist. He's seven and still deciding.

So as Kristen and I work with you through this book, you'll be tapping into years of experience, passion, trials, and errors.

We'll let you know what works (not just for us, but for the many people whose brains we've tapped into for this book), what doesn't, and how you can find yourself sitting smugly in a foreign café, bar, beach, or restaurant, living that wildly unpredictable life you always dreamed of. Being that person in the Facebook ad. Or being, quite simply, the person you always wanted to be in the place you always wanted to see.

So, I'll smugly settle back in my comfy chair in my heritage-listed house in my quiet village, nestled in the woods of the Elster Valley, take a sip of Irish Breakfast Tea, and see you in the next chapter!

A Post-Script: We are writing this book in changing times. Every day there is another story about a travel restriction, a change in visa requirements, or an update in documentation required to work or travel abroad. Therefore, we humbly ask for your understanding if some information you read here has changed or is no longer valid at the time of reading.

We do pledge to update these pages periodically as well as address the very latest developments in our Facebook group: Free At Last: Live, Love & Work Abroad. Please come and join the conversation!

In any case, the world changes so quickly. One thing that does not and will not change, however, is our shared humanity and shared right to peace, freedom, and opportunity.

Kristen and Jacqueline in Rentzschmühle, Germany. 2016.

CHAPTER 2: SHORT-TERM JOBS

*"Everything flows and nothing abides,
everything gives way and nothing stays fixed."*
–Hereclitus

CHOOSING YOUR DESTINATION AND GETTING WORK PERMISSION

Jacqueline

For me, it was always about Germany. We'd lived across Asia and the Pacific as children growing up, but when it came time to find my own place in the world, it was clear. Germany was calling my name, and so in 2004 I headed off for a working holiday.

Hold on, *working* holiday? Yes. Many countries offer these types of visas as a part of reciprocal agreements designed to encourage tourism and cultural exchanges, and although they open doors there are broad restrictions.

Let's start with the opening of doors: for me, I was under 30 and wanted to spend more than the usual 90 days abroad. I wanted to experience more of Berlin than the broad brush-strokes, explore the heartbeat of the city, and find the pulse beating my name. I applied at the local Embassy in Canberra, filling in the requisite forms, supplying requisite photographs and proof of savings, and within a short space of time was back again picking up my visa. The adventure could begin!

So those are the open doors – permission to stay longer than 90 days and permission to work. But what about the restrictions?

These vary somewhat, but broadly speaking:

- Working holiday visas are intended for **younger people**, generally between the ages of 18 – 30 (or in some cases 35);

- You may be **restricted** in the **type of work you can undertake**, and the **length of time** you are permitted to work for one employer. This is where the "holiday" part of the visa comes into play – essentially this visa is not intended for you to advance your career, rather to enable cultural exchange and a cultural connection. So yes, a holiday. The "working" part enables you to sustain a longer "holiday."

- You'll likely need to demonstrate that you **have sufficient funds** to support you while you're settling into your new life abroad, and looking for work. This requirement can entail showing a printed bank statement, or more onerous proof, and the required amount will differ from country to country. Essentially what is being determined here is can you look after yourself should you have difficulty finding work.

- You'll need to demonstrate that you **have health / travel insurance**, so that should you require medical or other assistance you'll be covered. This makes complete sense and I'm a huge fan of travel insurance.

  When I was 18 and in the USA I was involved in a car accident which fractured my spine, bunged up my neck and loosened all my teeth. The $258 which I paid for travel insurance paid my over $20,000 in medical expenses and flight home. A pretty good investment, I think you'll agree. Just like the old ads for American Express used to say, "don't leave home without it."

As of 2017 (my time of writing), these are the countries currently offering working holiday visas:

In **Africa**: South Africa.

In **Asia**: Bangladesh, Hong Kong, Indonesia, Israel, Japan, Malaysia, Philippines, Singapore, South Korea, Taiwan, Thailand, Turkey and Vietnam.

In **Europe**: Andorra, Austria, Belgium, Croatia, Cyprus, Czech Republic, Denmark, Estonia, Finland, France, Germany, Greece, Hungary, Iceland, Ireland, Italy, Latvia, Liechtenstein, Lithuania, Malta, Monaco, the Netherlands, Norway, Poland, Portugal, Romania, Russia, Slovakia, Slovenia, Spain, Sweden, Switzerland, Ukraine and the UK.

In **the Americas**: Argentina, Brazil, Canada, Chile, Colombia, Costa Rica, Mexico, Peru, Uruguay and the USA.

In **Oceania**: Australia and New Zealand.

So there's a pretty comprehensive list for you to country-shop through. The finer details for working holiday visas can be found via Embassy websites, so you can let your fingers do the walking – or you could use Wikipedia as a starting point before honing in on the finer details.

Note: You'll need to check that your country has a reciprocal working holiday visa agreement with the country of your choice!

Perhaps there's a country that calls your name, as Germany did mine. If you don't speak the local language, don't let that dissuade you. Languages are an adventure to learn, as much an insight into culture as cuisine, music, and sport. In fact, did you know recent studies show that the language you speak can influence the way you view the world? Pretty fascinating stuff!

Jacqueline enjoying Berlin, Germany during World Cup 2006.

Jacqueline's Tips For "More Seasoned" (AKA: Spicy) Travellers

"But I'm older than 35!" I hear you say. Don't despair – the ship hasn't sailed though I'd be lying if I said it wasn't as easy. Like you, I'm on the other side of 35. In fact, at the time of writing I've got birthday number 41 knocking on the door (deep breaths, deep breaths!) So what are the options for over-35s? Put on your wanderlust boots and get trekking through these ideas…

- **WWOOF**: no, I'm not making a strange dog sound, rather referring to Willing Workers On

Organic Farms, also known as World Wide Opportunities on Organic Farms. In return for up to 6 hours work per day, you get free accommodation, food, travel possibilities and an unbelievable chance to really get to know a region, a culture, and your host family. If you visit the WWOOF website (wwoofinternatoinal.org) you can explore options suitable to your interests and abilities.

- **TESOL / TEFL**: I know, I know – you were waiting until I'd come around to Teaching English to Speakers of Other Languages (also referred to as Teaching English as a Foreign Language). Surely this has to be a popular pathway to travel abroad, and is one that rewards those of us with more experience under our belt, longer in the professional tooth.

  The world can be your oyster once you're TESOL-certified, though my word of warning would be to look carefully at options and inclusions when contemplating taking up a position abroad. Your first step would be to get qualified, ensuring that your qualification is recognized internationally.

  A quick Google search for "TESOL certificate" or "CELTA" should get you in the right direction. Plus then there are websites like ESL Base that list job opportunities. I find ESL

Base to be reputable, though please let me know if your experience is any different!

- **Boat Crew:** Land ahoy! Sorry, I couldn't help myself... Now, if you're a land lubber like me, this option for working abroad might not be your cup of tea, but if the idea of salt spray and the rolling waves gets your blood racing, and if you've got some experience on the seas, then this might be an opportunity for you. You'll need to be able to offer something to a shop or yacht's crew, and be willing to work hard (and to learn on the way), so if that tickles your fancy you could check out sites such as Offshore Passage Opportunities or Workaway.

- **Help Exchange**: exchanging your volunteering skills for accommodation and food could be your ticket around the world. And there's a bonus – it can do your heart good! Whereas WWOOF is about volunteering on farms and living on the land, Help Exchange goes one step further and could see you working in a community centre, building a school, working with animals, caring for children... there are a plethora of opportunities for the hard-working volunteer. Let us know how it goes!

So there you have it – some opportunities for the over-35s amongst us to live the dream of working and travelling abroad, all the while knowing we can go home any time we're ready to.

Expat Tales: Elvis "elvo" Kibiti -Kenyan Who Used to Live in the USA, Now Living in China

"I was born and raised in Meru, Kenya (18 years), moved to California for college, and spent 12 years split between Los Angeles (two years) and the San Francisco area (ten years), and have now been living in Shanghai, China for the last five years.

My move to China was as a result of the job I held in San Francisco at a tech company. I used to make five or so trips annually to China for business and decided to move to China to try my hand at the expat thing.

Living in China has been one of the best experiences of my life. As diverse as the US is, people tend to live very segregated lives, which is completely different from us "immigrants" in China.

I have met so many people from a variety of age groups, countries, professions, etc. If you were to take age group as an example, in the US you won't find 22 year-olds going to the same bars/ events etc. with 65 year-olds or even 40 year-olds. This is pretty much the norm living abroad in

China. Everyone hangs out with everyone regardless.

If you like to travel and like to experience different things I would recommend that you try living away from your home country in a heartbeat.

When you are first planning on leaving you will feel compelled to save your belongings, put them in storage, etc. and keep them intact for your very imminent return.

However, as soon as you hit the one year mark away, you forget about your belongings and the thought of going back to deal with them becomes more of a burden as your mindset switches to wanting to live abroad longer.

My advice, when you decide you want to live abroad is to get rid of your belongings and assume you won't be moving back! Pack light and forget about accumulating physical things as you won't have room for those with all the memories and experiences that will take their place."

Soothing The Naysayers and Your Own Nerves

Kristen

Let's pause for a moment to check in with our own apprehensions. Perhaps you've already told your lofty plans to family and friends and received a less than enthusiastic response or even outright objections.

They may have told you that in fact you "cannot work abroad! It's too dangerous. -Too risky. Only bad things can happen because of the fact you want to go alone, or because you are a female (or black, disabled, Jewish, gay, etc.), and there's crime, terrorism, and so on."

You may have even allowed their fears to become your own. This is natural and perfectly understandable. Change can be scary. The unknown is scary. And sometimes we tend to listen to the loudest voices rather than the most supportive or reasonable.

Now it would be outright wrong of me to say that nothing bad could happen to you if you decide to live and work abroad for a short or long-term spell. But I also couldn't promise you'd be safe sitting home playing video games in your parents' basement either. (There are always earthquakes, falling meteorites, and mind-controlling aliens disguised as game consoles to think about!)

People prefer "the devil they know vs. the one they don't know" right? It's human nature.

When I was working as a university student one summer in Provincetown, Massachusetts, I had a

Northern Irish coworker from Belfast whose parents were terrified that she was in the USA. "Don't go *there*. All the crime! The shootings! The murders!" they chorused. Meanwhile, I was planning on visiting Belfast in the year ahead and my American parents and grandparents chided me saying, "Don't go *there*. It's dangerous. You will get blown up."

Isn't it funny how similar everyone is the world over? Both our families were worried about the dangers from "out there" and urging us both to "stay here where it is safe."

Obviously I don't recommend you go traipsing around a warzone or down a dark alley in a major world city at 2AM in your halter-top and mini skirt. You have to learn as much as you can about where you are going, take precautions to be safe, and use your good old common sense.

My Northern Irish friend never travelled alone and only visited big cities like New York sparingly and with a group of friends. When I went to Belfast, I took a three day Paddywagon Tour from Dublin with other twenty-somethings, was in and out in a few days, and had a ball.

I'm also not implying that you should ignore or make light of your loved ones' fears. They love you after all! But do weigh their concerns with your own research, level-headedness, and ability to make a sound decision as a fully-grown adult.

BEFORE YOU GO: FUNDING YOUR "WORKING HOLIDAY OR SHORT-TERM STINT ABROAD"

Kristen

Repeat after me. "Thou shall not travel abroad without any money. Thou shall not show up to a new country homeless and destitute."

If you are independently wealthy, I suppose you can skip this section. The rest of us need to keep our wits about us so we can make our dreams of international travel and living/working/volunteering abroad an actual reality.

It may sound strange that you would need to work so that you can then work abroad. Of course you will need the means to feed yourself and a place to stay while you are looking for work in your new host country. The best way to do this is have a supply of cash that can keep you going for at *least* a month, preferably three to six months or more in the event you have trouble getting a job.

You should also always have at least enough money to get back home just in case! Don't expect your country's embassy, helpful as they can be, to bail you out and pick up your return ticket for free in the event of an emergency.

If you somehow have the opportunity to secure work in your new host country before you arrive (such as with a prearranged paid internship), by all means, take it! Unfortunately for most people, especially twenty-somethings with short-term working holiday visas or similar, you just have to arrive and find work once you have landed.

I've done some pretty embarrassing yet character-building things to successfully ensure I had enough survival money before embarking on my two "working holidays" after graduating from Massachusetts College of Art and Design back in 1998.

No, thankfully I did not take up pole dancing, though working as a temp secretary for a Private (Pervert) Investigator in Southeastern Massachusetts a few weeks before flying to Dublin, Ireland was no less shady. (I'll give you that particular dirt in just a moment...)

My working visa for Ireland (valid for four months) was obtained from Council on International Educational Exchange (CIEE). A nonprofit, nongovernmental organization, CIEE is the USA's oldest and largest nonprofit study abroad and intercultural exchange organization. I also had secured a six-month working visa for the UK thanks to BUNAC, an organization that offers a range of exciting work abroad and volunteer abroad programs.

So with the bureaucracy of getting work permission behind me, I then had the more mundane problem of figuring out how to pay for my plane tickets and make sure I could eat and survive in my new host countries.

I decided to enlist with a temp agency in the Swansea/Fall River area in Massachusetts after begrudgingly moving back in with my parents at the age of 21 after four years of freewheeling freedom as a student in Boston. My goal was to save up a few hundred bucks over the summer to help protect against being "down and out" on the streets of Dublin. I was about to show up without either a place to live or a job after all! The plan was to try and obtain both within my first week of arrival in Ireland, and hopefully maybe even make a friend or two.

My part of Massachusetts where I'd grown up had been in an economic slump for quite some time so despite the fact I now had a shiny new college degree (albeit in *Painting* of all things,) the only jobs readily available through the temp agency were mainly of the factory or fast food variety.

So what was my very first job right out of university then? "Professor Palana" was a hired hand on an assembly line making just a little over minimum wage in **a birdfeeder factory** in Warren, Rhode Island -and it remains one of the toughest jobs I've ever had to this day!

This should have been my first clue that the year ahead in my life was to be like no other. Birdfeeder-assembler Kristen was to learn from a dizzying array of bad short-term jobs in the USA, Ireland, and later

Scotland what it means to slave all day long controlled by bells, punch-clocks, and insecure bosses desperate to assert their authority lest it be snatched away. I would be a cog in someone else's grand machine and not be paid a fair price for stifling my restless soul in exchange for quick and mindless labor that perhaps already is being done today (or soon enough) by robots.

I have nothing but respect for factory workers, mind you. (My parents met working in a factory in Fall River, MA. back in the 1960s.) I was humbled by the kind, down-to-earth folks I met at that first post-graduate job.

For them, working as quickly as humanly possible translated into a few cents extra they could earn for their families per hour. They warmly invited me on their monthly bus excursion to gamble those same pennies away at *Foxwoods Casino* in Connecticut and praised my superior cardboard box preparing abilities with "Good stamping Kristen!" I wish I could go back in time right now and hug them all. For it remains to this day that of all the people I've met around the world then and now, the very kindest have always been the ones with the least to share.

But alas, as fond as I was of the workers, I was also secretly full of myself with my new university degree and wanted to do something that used a little more of my brain. So I abruptly quit the factory job and got the secretary job for the Private Investigator instead from the temp agency a few days later.

My soon-to-be new boss enthusiastically commented "nice legs!" right before my job interview. (I was wearing a knee-length skirt.) He had been in the papers a few weeks prior for soliciting a prostitute. His workdays were spent taking cases trying to prove marital infidelity or underage sexual shenanigans by spying on his nervous clients' spouses and/or children. I would type up in reports what sordid activities he witnessed in his parked car through residential windows or whom he saw entering and leaving hotel parking lots and at which times.

He said he'd ditch the temp agency and pay me under the table if I wouldn't tell them I accepted a job with him so he'd save money and I'd make more. So I doubled my factory-worker's salary and had some sultry stories to amuse myself with typing away in his office to boot. By the time August and my flight to Dublin rolled around, I had a stash of (ill-begotten?) cash to help cushion my upcoming adventures.

What does all of this have to do with you? I suppose my main point is that sometimes (most times) you need to make sacrifices to make your dreams of international travel and living abroad come true.

For me it was to take short-term, non career-advancing temporary work to make the quick cash needed to then sustain me as I got set up in my adopted host country.

Again, I suppose if you are independently wealthy you can skip this step, though you may miss out on some mind-expanding experience and insights. (Or maybe you can buy someone else's?)

Some ideas for making survival money in a short amount of time include:

- **Sign up with your local Temp Agency.** Most of the work assignments will be in an office environment so having some typing skills is useful. However, depending on where you live, other types of skilled and unskilled jobs may be available.

- **Get a regular part time (or full time) job.** Then put in your two weeks' notice right before you need to leave. Here in most cases you'll have to keep your short-term work intentions to yourself as most bosses-to-be won't be interested in hiring and then having to replace you just a few short weeks or months after you start.

- **Do some "under the table" odd jobs.** Consider helping family, friends, and neighbors with tasks such as lawn care/landscaping, house painting, babysitting, repair work, snow shoveling, shopping/helping with errands, driving, etc.

- **Look for seasonal work in the local or online papers.** Is your local mall looking for a part-time Santa (or Mrs. Claus) or people to wrap gifts for customers? Or maybe the local amusement park is hiring for the summer? This could be a nice short-term option and no need to feel guilty for leaving after a few weeks.

- **Dip your toe in the online "sharing" economy.** Share your talents and skills by doing freelance work (via websites like *Fiverr* or *Upwork*), create a course that teaches others what you know (through websites like *Udemy, Skillshare,* etc.) or do consulting or teaching through live *Skype* sessions.

  Please note that it can take some time to see a return on your time and energy investment with most of these sites. So do give them a try, but preferably in combination with something else like an in-person, location-based job.

- **Save money from your current job.** If you have more than a few weeks or months to prepare for your working holiday, set aside a set amount each payday at your current job to finance your excursion. The more time you have, the more you can save, even if it's just $10 a week. Little things add up.

- **Crowdfunding.** I cover this more extensively in *Chapter 3: Volunteer Work and Internships Abroad.* I also have a fun, accessible, and easy to use book on this very topic that can get you up and running in about one hour and raising hundreds to thousands of dollars ASAP for your trip: *Crowdfunding Confidential: Raise Money For You and Your Cause*.

Jacqueline

Thanks, Kristen! Unfortunately, when I set out to conquer the world, not only had I never heard of Crowdfunding, I was also painfully shy around the themes of money. Mine wasn't a noble journey, rather an escape from… something.

Okay, if I'm completely honest it was an escape from me. This is a topic that I'm working on in a separate project, but my impetus in leaving Australia was to make critical changes to who I was. And that's something I could only admit to myself in those quiet moments in the middle of the night, and working to get myself away was something I could only undertake myself. In fact, it wasn't until I'd booked and paid for my tickets that I let family and friends know I was going away, so personal was the decision.

In a nutshell, I was suffering from Generalised Anxiety Disorder and its bedfellow, depression. I was incredibly unhappy and unstable but was also high functioning, so I worked my patootie off to cover up the fact that I was fracturing on the inside, with every day little pieces splintering away. I could see myself from the outside, and didn't like what I saw – despite the professional successes, and so with determination I decided that the only way to save myself was to have a complete, 100 percent change of scenery... to utterly change my lifestyle.

So I self-funded my trip abroad: from Monday to Friday I continued coordinating branding projects at the City of Melbourne, and on Saturdays and Sundays I'd drive across town to sit in a display home in the middle of a new housing development, handing out brochures to interested new home owners. Working seven days a week for a couple of months was draining, but I had the golden goal in mind: my flight and some cash to keep me afloat.

Flash forward to today, and I can assure you – the plan worked. The complete change of scenery acted like a reset button. Invigorated, refreshed, relaxed and strong, working and travelling abroad changed my life. But, we cover all that in more detail throughout the book! Let's keep on.

It might take a few months or it might take a year or longer. It took hard work, but it was worth it in the end.

So, my advice, if you're doing this on your own?

- **Set realistic saving goals, and stick to them**
  After all – the new shoes or jacket can wait!

- **Set up a separate bank account for your savings**
  Some banks offer higher interest earning accounts that can be linked to your normal savings account. If you can, make regular payments or transfers into the Holiday Saver

(let's call it that, for fun!), and try to forget it's there. That money should be untouchable until you go away.

- **See what you can sell**
  If you're planning on going away for an extended period, are you going to put your belongings into storage, leave them with friends, or earn some extra cash from them? If you're not particularly attached to your bed, fridge and so on, pop it on *eBay, Gumtree, Craig's List,* or into your local classifieds. As they say in the *Tesco* ads, "every little helps."

If I – a profligate spender and lover of fine dining – can squirrel away enough to buy a plane ticket and have spare change, so can you.

And as I said, the change was completely worth it for my mental and physical health. So – what are you going to do today to get your savings off the ground?

FINDING TEMPORARY AND SHORT-TERM WORK OPPORTUNITIES

Kristen

So, after your plane has just landed in your new host country, the first thing you'll want to do after checking into your youth hostel (sorry, if you don't have a job yet you're better off skipping the five-star hotel) is hit the ground running and start looking for jobs ASAP.

Common sense tips for recent graduates I could have used when I first arrived in Dublin:

You just graduated from university? Good for you. Well done. Now get over yourself! You are *not* here in your new country to necessarily advance your career or pay off your student loans in a month.

You are here for the experience of becoming more self-reliant, more worldly, and experiencing a new country and culture up close and personal. Do *not* get all "uppity" and thumb your nose at menial and manual jobs that do not require higher education. In fact, since you are most likely only working for a few months, you can't really expect to get your dream job, the corner office and the starting salary at $75K+ straight away. Most countries would prefer their *own* citizens get such employment anyway if you catch my drift. Like it or not, you'll soon be a foreigner in another land and will be subject to being treated like one, for better or worse.

If your friends back home were lucky enough to find work straight out of university, good for them. Life is not a race or competition and you will have plenty of time for your career and ladder climbing once you eventually return home.

I mention this because I had trouble after arrival in Dublin accepting the fact that though I was *so sure* I was destined for greatness, I was making less than $3USD an hour as an overworked waitress in a sports bar. Bonus life lesson: In Ireland and most of Europe there is almost no culture of tipping wait staff like in the US so don't count on living off your tips to make your rent payments!

So in my four short months in one of my all-time favorite countries, I wasted far too much time fussing and worrying, working and quitting, searching and finding replacement jobs, only to work and quit again and again. I held and left a total of six jobs in a very short amount of time!

By the time I got to Edinburgh, Scotland I finally calmed down, found a job in a game and electronics shop and stayed for the duration of my 6-month visa. Maybe it helped that I knew I soon was heading back to the USA for graduate school in New York City and had to enjoy the present situation abroad while I had the chance. Ah. Life is so much easier when you don't fight with the experiences life wants you to have.

So, back to just arriving in your new country… Where do you find that first job straight away?

A few of the many places you can start looking include:

- **The bulletin board of your youth hostel or guesthouse**. You may also find potential roommates or apartments for rent here as well. (Yes, while looking for a job, you'll also want to find a place to live. Staying in a hotel, youth hostel, or guest house is usually meant to be temporary until you find your footing.)

- **The organization where you got your work visa.** They often have an office location in your new host city where you can go and view their bulletin boards or use their computers or career center to find short-term work.

- **The usual suspects online.** Try the local searches by city/country available via *Craigslist, Monster, LinkedIn, Idealist.org,* and others. Many countries also have their own local online job boards so do spend time doing your research.

- **Word of mouth**. Do *not* "poo poo" this underrated but powerful offline option! (I owe almost my entire career to word of mouth leads mixed with a healthy dose of being in the right place at the right time.) You're likely to find others in the youth hostel or guesthouse who also came to work. Did they just find a job somewhere? They are still hiring? Great! Follow up on any leads you get.

- **Local schools and universities.** You may not be able to take advantage of their career centers as those are often reserved exclusively for their own students. However, if you can walk around campus you are likely to find random flyers and postings for short-term jobs.

- **Temp Agencies**. These are always a great resource, especially for those of you who prefer office work to shop and restaurant jobs.

- **The "cold" email, call, or walk-in.** OK. This is a bit brash but it has worked for me on many occasions. See a place you'd like to work but they don't seem to be hiring? First do your research on their goals and needs to see how you might fit into the puzzle. Then send them an email with your resume/CV and explain how you could potentially help them out with your particular skills and talents!

If you are feeling especially bold, you might even just walk in off the street and see if you can speak with a manager or the owner. (I got my first gallery job in Fall River, MA. at age 18, my first painting studio in Dublin at age 22, and my most recent university job here in Myanmar just a few months ago the very same way!)

Too shy for this trick? Me too. I am the biggest introvert you will ever meet, but thankfully I have the ability to temporarily *act* like an extrovert when I am teaching, looking for a job, or when meeting new people. "Fake it until you make it" as they say. You can always hide in your bed later with a flashlight and a good book to recover your energies.

- **Post your own job and let people contact you.** For this you'll have to check your email often or get a local phone number/ SIM card and cell phone.

Can you help with informal English conversational skills? Could you babysit while teaching English or another language to local kids? (Parents everywhere LOVE the concept of finding childcare together with foreign language immersion for their little darlings.) Do you have special skills with computers, music, art, or anything else that might be in demand in your new locale? Make sure to advertise and let people know that you are the one they have been waiting for.

Just one more important thing: Obviously the kind of work you can find and get will depend on your own unique skills and qualifications, which country you are in, what their attitude towards foreigners is, and your level and understanding of the local language.

If your language skills in your new country are not substantial enough to allow you to take orders in a café for example, you may still be able to wash dishes back in the kitchen. If you are an English speaker, you'll often be able to find many formal and informal ways to make money helping others learn your native language. Just make sure that if you decide to go this route you take this very meaningful work seriously! You may even want to have a look at Jacqui's awesome how-to book, <u>Teaching English: Your Guide to Launching a Successful ESL Teaching Career</u>.

Expat Tales: Brie Casazza -American Living in Germany

"I didn't have a job when I moved to Germany. I spent my first six months learning the language and doing a bit of traveling in the country. When my funds were getting low, I decided to look for work. I walked into the office of the language school off the street and asked if they needed an English trainer – a very American move, I would learn. My luck was that they did.

I worked freelance for about the first month, but to get a work visa, the Foreigners Office insisted I have a full-time contract. The school director wanted to keep me on, so he gave me what I needed to stay. After three years of full-time employment, I was given an unlimited residence and working permit."

Jacqueline

Now, not that I have any direct experience on this score but there are whispers and rumours of what has been done before, and these are what I'd like to share with you. (Actually, they're real stories, but I'm just trying to sound mysterious).

These are jobs which aren't going to make you rich, but they'll put food in your belly and a roof over your head, and extend that holiday just a little bit longer. And who knows, something official could come out of it. And if not, at least wild stories to scare (or share with) the grand-kiddies one day.

I want to preface all of this by saying that, in my humble opinion, the one government agency you never want to get on the wrong side of is the Tax Office. Think of your home country and what happens when there's undeclared income or unpaid tax. It's not pretty, right? So please take any information here with a heavy pinch of salt – it's for information purposes only and may help you out of a bind, but it's no long-term replacement for (what I loosely call, knowing you'll understand) "real work."

So, where can we start with "off the books" work? The easiest place is, naturally, in the pub. Or, to be more precise, the hospitality industry. Now I'm talking outback bars, ski field pubs, local restaurants, hotels, hostels, and resorts. In this field, you're limited only by your sassiness, grit, determination, and aversion to alcohol-induced mayhem. If you catch my drift!

How does it work? If you're looking for some short-term financial plus points to sustain your holiday, approach local pubs, bars and restaurants in your locale. Ask if there's any need for some extra hands, let them know your availability, and see what happens. If you're in a country where your native language isn't the foreign tongue, bar and pub work will get you fluent in no time. Nothing quite like necessity to kick your language acquisition in the pants!

You might also find that your hostel is looking for workers – cleaners, bar staff, reception, etc. In exchange accommodation might be gratis or there might be a meal or two in it for you. Certainly it doesn't hurt to ask when you check in, or even send the hostelling association an email before you arrive.

So that's something to add to the checklist. But what else? Babysitting is one option, but keep in mind this is a longer-term commitment, not something for a weekend or couple of weeks. Babysitting involves a huge amount of trust, and you have to be trustworthy. Keep in mind there's an increasing number of international agencies that facilitate au pairs and nannies (definitely vetted and often age-restricted positions), so babysitting is something you're more likely to pick up through friends, friends of friends, or mutual connections.

If travels have taken you to the shores, you could find some day work at the docks working on ships or yachts. This work is for the physical amongst you, and if the captain says there's painting, polishing, sanding, mending, cleaning, or varnishing to be done, agree on the rate and get those sleeves rolled up. Me hearty!

There's one more type of work I wanted to touch on here, and this is one which shouldn't require a working visa because, essentially, you're working and earning money in your home country, even whilst abroad. It's freelance work via <u>Fiverr</u>. Fiverr is, in my opinion, *the* site for digital nomads, freelancers with itchy feet, and entrepreneurs on the go. I've been a Fiverr freelancer, taking advantage of those spare moments between my real-life teaching work and volunteering to earn some extra euros writing travel articles and proof-reading theses.

It's free to set up a profile on Fiverr and to offer "gigs", and with fixed prices per offer, a 10% fee (accurate at time of writing) per gig and no-fuss payments direct into your PayPal account, I reckon this is one option to keep in mind when on the road. Of course you'll need reliable Internet and a laptop or tablet sufficient to complete the work you're offering, but this is work you can do when it suits you. What could be better when travelling, right?

Expat Tales: Sweety -Indian Living in the USA

"I came to the USA for higher studies when I was 22. I had no family here in the USA, only a few friends that I knew from back home. I came to study Electrical Engineering.

I saw that all the students worked to support their lifestyles while still in school and college. Now, working while studying was a totally new concept for me. In India, most of the students, regardless of their age, don't work if they are studying.

As an international student, I was allowed to work only 20 hours a week, which at the beginning was a lot of hours for me because I had never ever dreamed of working while studying!

The student center in my college advised that I should look for some student aid job on the campus.

One day I was roaming around the mall near campus and I saw a candy cart right in the center of the mall. It was very colorful and attractive which made me stop by the store. I saw the owner was working there whose accent sounded so familiar from the region where I was from. I asked him and he was from the same town in India that I was from!

We started chatting and he said he needed some help with his store. If I could help him, he would pay me some money in return. (It had to be cash because I couldn't work until I had all the paperwork set up. That was an illegal job because it was paid in cash without reporting to the government.) I didn't know much about the rules of working without the proper paperwork because most of the people do cash jobs in India.

I started working at the candy store. I was very excited to deal with the American people, since this was the very first time I was going to communicate with lots of Americans in a day.

My first day was learning about all kinds of different candies and the other products that they had. It was so much fun until it was time to close the store. I was asked to mop the floor and change the garbage bag. I was in a shock!

While growing up, I never did such things. We had maids to do this work. I never even took my plate to the kitchen after eating, or did dishes or any household work for my own self. I was spoiled I guess.

I asked, 'Why would I mop the floor and touch the dirty garbage? That's not my job. You should have some other person doing that.' And the answer that I got was, 'Welcome to America! Here people do everything on their own unless they are filthy rich. Get used to doing all the chores on your own.'

That brought tears to my eyes and gave me the first bitter experience of working in another country. I couldn't argue since it was the very first day ever. I silently did mop the floor and changed the garbage bag. For a few days after, I constantly thought of quitting because I was not at all comfortable working like that.

I was selling in the store, keeping track of inventory and mopping the floor, and was extremely underpaid (roughly the American minimum wage.) I left the job within a few days because of my dissatisfaction. But this is also a very easy way to let someone take advantage of you since you can't report them for paying you almost nothing and having to do so much work."

Kristen

At first I had forgotten those times when I've been paid "under the table" both at home and abroad and now I realize that I do have some stories and advice to share. Again as Jacqueline says, all to be taken with a heavy pinch of salt!

For one, speaking of pubs, you remember I was living in Ireland right? How could I *not* have a pub story for you?

They used to call me "Half Pint," "One Drink Wonder," and on a good day, "Two Can Sam." Yes, I'm afraid I am not so talented in the drinking arts. After a half pint of stout or beer, I really have no desire to drink any more. After spending some time in Dublin, my tolerance built up to just about two pints. (These days I'm lucky if I can finish just one!)

Social life, especially in one's twenties tends to revolve around the pub in Ireland and in the UK so what would I do after my drink was done to while away the hours with friends in the pub? I would draw in my sketchbook!

You wouldn't think one could make money with a humble sketchbook but you'd be wrong. I would often draw the musicians or other pub-goers. People would walk by and look over my shoulder shouting compliments and encouragement. Then one day a (drunk?) passer-by asked if he could buy my drawing.

"Um. OK?" I replied timidly.

Whoosh. Before I knew it he had handed me 20 quid (Euros weren't around yet) and I was carefully tearing that page out of my sketchbook.

So yes, I'm all about appeasing the tax man or woman, but this was one of those situations where it really didn't seem necessary.

After a few more similar incidents in the pub, I got it in my head to start drawing portraits on Grafton St. (I hear that these days you need a permit, FYI.) And so with my easel, paper pad, pens, and two milk crates given to me by a kindly Dublin street vendor, (one for me, one for the customers to sit on) I had my very first thriving, albeit under-the table art-making business!

Kristen, age 22 in 1998. -Street Portraits in Dublin, Ireland.

These days I still make artwork for people, but I do things properly. I pay "Self Employment Tax," have clients sign contracts before I begin, and charge them via an invoicing system hooked up to my trusty PayPal account.

But if I were just randomly making a painting or drawing and someone came up and offered to give me money for it... Well. Say no more!

WE'RE NOT IN KANSAS ANYMORE: DEALING WITH THE DIFFERENCES

Jacqueline

Not all Germans wear Lederhosen? Disappointing! Sausages and beer for breakfast? Now that is interesting... Yes, cultural differences can go both ways, and discovering your personal positives and negatives (and breaking point) is part of the joy of working abroad.

For me, cultural differences around formality continue to be challenging. What do I mean?

Working at the City of Melbourne, we called our CEO by his first name, David, as we did with our Director (Scott) and Manager (Mary). The Lord Mayor, (John So) however, was always referred to as "Lord Mayor."

We wore flats or high heels, loud jewellery or none at all, and although we were casual in our use of titles we were professional in our dealings with the stakeholders, the media, and in our written communication. This innate balance between informality and professionalism comes naturally to (most) Australians, and informality is a part of our culture.

Coming to Germany where you'll find colleagues who've worked together more than 20 years still referring to one another as "Herr Schmidt" and "Frau Müller," who don't share Friday after-work drinks, and who would never use the informal "Du" (you) form when speaking, was a huge culture shock. It may sound ridiculous, but it was something significant which I had to get used to in order to integrate successfully into the working culture. As I write, though, I realise that I still struggle with this aspect of my adopted culture.

For some people it's an easy thing to adjust to, however other cultural aspects might be more difficult – bureaucracy, road rules, recycling, pets in restaurants, the placement of cutlery on the plate to indicate a meal is finished, taxes, compulsory military service, lack of accessible entries to government buildings, ticket inspectors on trains who don't and can't sell tickets, and so on.

I write this as a reminder that when we live and work abroad, we need to adjust our expectations, update our norms, accept differences and see them as interesting rather than negative. This is your new normal. Sure, some cultural norms might really grate, but we're not working abroad with the expectation that everything is going to be the same as back home, right? We're in it for the complete immersive experience.

Here are my top tips for dealing with cultural differences:

- **Have and retain your sense of humour**
  Nothing quite says "I'm comfortable with myself and where I am in the world" quite like smiling

inwardly through your new norms. Differences can challenge, but they don't need to break us.

- **At work: establish whether a specific behaviour is a requirement of your job**
There are some cultural differences which you will have to accept and adjust to if you want to be successful at your job, and some which you don't. Decide where you need to adjust your behavior or expectations, and accept this adjustment as your new norm.

- **At work: decide whether or not you can reasonably accommodate a particular cultural difference**
For example, let's consider communication: In your new home, how can employers and employees provide feedback to one another? How direct or forthright can one speak to colleagues when discussing differences or addressing conflict? How is praise given?

- **Learn about other cultures**
Kristen and I have both advised to learn before you go, or at least to learn on the go. When prepared for difference (whether that be related to communication, the physical environment, or culinary) you'll be more aware of where you may need to alter your practices.

- **Ask questions**
Before making sweeping statements about a country, city, locality, person or people, song,

food item, or ticket machine, ask questions. Opening our ears and minds can reveal unexpected titbits of information and insights that can help us better understand our new home, and better adjust to her differences.

Let's hear from Heather about what it was like for her.

Expat Tales: Heather LaBonte Efthymiou - American Living in Cyprus, Formerly in the UK

"When I moved to the UK it was very difficult for me to find either administrative work or a job working with children. In the USA, in my experience up to 2006, experience was enough to find jobs in either field. In the UK they want you to have special qualifications for even receptionist jobs! I began to really dislike the word qualifications.

In California I had worked on the executive floor of Apple. In the UK I could not even get a receptionist job. One thing I learned in the UK is that the British love paperwork and lots of it.

I ended up having to settle for an awful job in a call center, which was depressing to say the least. Our bathroom breaks were timed and limited. It was a crazy situation. I was not used to working somewhere where I needed to ask to use the bathroom and then had to run to said bathroom and do my business as fast as possible.

Also, we lived in the city with limited parking so I had no car. It was a new thing for me to have to trek to bus stops (even in the snow) and take buses that were full to brimming. Also, I am sensitive to cigarette smoke and smoking was allowed in most places when I first moved to the UK. In California I had the luxury, for many years, of no cigarette smoke allowed in most places. This may sound silly to some but, if it causes health issues, it is a very real bother."

CULTURAL DIFFERENCES, DIPLOMACY, AND DISCRIMINATION

Kristen

In 1999 in Edinburgh, Scotland one of my very organized and capable English female coworkers (at a video game store on Princess Street) told me she wanted to apply for an assistant manager position. She was turned down by our so-called superiors (all male) and given the reason that she was "too girly" for the job. Seriously? I mean couldn't they have at least come up with some other excuse? It's one thing to be sexist, but that was just downright lazy.

Only a few weeks later my home country (USA) happened to be bombing my boss's country (Serbia.) My very annoyed and justifiably flustered boss ordered me to "Hoover (vacuum) the store" because I was "American as well as a girl."

Obviously your race, gender, religion, sexual orientation, country of origin, or (insert label of choice here) can and may very well be a factor in how you are treated working abroad as well as at home.

My advice is to first, try and understand before you even arrive the cultural norms, customs, and attitudes that are prevalent in your host country by doing a bit of reading and research. You may not agree with how things are done for example in Saudi Arabia, but at least you also won't show up as a woman expecting to be hired as a taxi driver either! (*For those who have not had the occasion to research, women are currently not allowed to legally drive in Saudi Arabia.)

I would also suggest that when you do encounter discrimination abroad, especially when you are there for only a short amount of time, that you do allow *some* things to roll off your back and that you pick your battles wisely. My Italian boss at a coffee shop I worked at briefly in Dublin used to tease me in front of customers. "Oh! Sorry about the lack of foam on your cappuccino Signore. She's an *American*." I would just laugh and roll my eyes at the customer and say, "Can you believe this guy?"

My general response to these types of low-grade, essentially harmless personal jibes was to fight back with humor while also calling them out on their bogus comments. For example, in Scotland my Serbian boss and I actually got on quite well despite the awkwardness of our two countries being at odds. I told him that I would vacuum the store "because it was my job, not because of Bill Clinton."

"And tomorrow I want to see Scott over here do it instead of picking his nose at the cash register." I'd added. (Incidentally Scott got fired a month later for swiping cash from that very same cash register. He should have stuck with picking his nose. My bad!)

On the other hand, I encouraged and helped my aspiring assistant manager friend in Scotland to report and fight the sexist discrimination she was subject to. And she did. And she won.

Pick your battles wisely especially when you are just in the host country for a few weeks or months. You can also always fight behind the scenes by helping embolden and empower those who will be remaining in your host country.

You are going to be working abroad for a full cultural immersion and no doubt you will experience the good as well as the bad wherever you go. Most discrimination hides in plain view in the form or a joke or random comment (with some people even completely unaware of their own prejudices) and here you can decide how forcefully you will respond or if you will even respond at all.

Do remember that wherever you go, you will encounter people without the same opportunities as you to travel and experience diverse cultures and peoples. Many may have been immersed in a particular worldview their entire lives and so you may be their very first exposure (besides what they've seen on TV or online) to something new. Therefore, how you respond and interact will likely affect how they view others like you moving forward. I personally always err on the side of being friendly and diplomatic rather than defensive or antagonistic. I aspire as much as possible to take the high road always with the hopes of changing a deeply engrained perception or challenging an outdated stereotype.

Of course by no means should you ever tolerate more serious forms of abuse such as actual threats or violence! As long as you are using common sense (not walking alone in a dark alley at 3AM, respecting cultural norms, avoiding people who give you bad vibes, etc.) then you should rarely if ever experience such horrors. Do however seek medical help, the aid of law enforcement, and the services of your country's embassy in the event of an actual emergency!

If you really are experiencing heavy discrimination, harassment, or anything that makes you miserable on a daily basis, remember to love yourself first and move on your merry way to a better situation ASAP. Then after the dust has settled, share your experience with others in the form of a blog post, book, artwork, or film to help raise awareness and/or warn others. Don't let that bad experience go to waste!

Jacqueline

In writing this book I've had ample opportunity to look around my home, through decades of photographs sparking innumerable memories, and to reflect on the ins and outs of life abroad. This topic of cultural differences, discrimination, and diplomacy has, to be honest, left me spinning a little. Perhaps I choose to see the best in the world? Delete negative experiences, or ignore them completely? My parents raised us with the unwavering belief that regardless of skin colour, religion, language, gender, sexuality, race, ethnicity, income, and opportunity, we are all equal. We bleed the same, laugh the same, cry the same, and love the same.

But, of course, the ideal isn't the rule in daily life, as we all know too well.

Kristen gave some great examples of discrimination based on gender and nationality, and on those notes there's not much more I can add. However, I am reminded of workplace discrimination which some friends experienced, and these experiences should serve as "red flags" for you when working abroad.

An American friend of mine was working here in Germany as a freelance English teacher for the local franchise of an internationally renowned school, and it was his first time in such a job.

He'd recently finished University, had qualified as a TESOL trainer, and was here living with his German girlfriend. After a short while he was offered a permanent contract with the school, which was a fabulous opportunity as it gave him security with his visa. So, all was happy and good. Until the teaching hours crept up to well over what was written in the contract. And translation jobs were added on top of that. And it was revealed that in the wording of his contract, he was given "at least" x hours of teaching, not "up to" x hours of teaching. Meaning it was limitless. He was teaching over 40 units per week, so add in 20 hours' preparation time plus translation / proofreading time and he was barely sleeping. He wasn't allowed leave, and the freelance trainers in the school were not permitted to offer him relief by taking over teaching hours.

So my friend became ill, completely burned out, and took a medical break. He was harassed with phone calls daily, called a liar and a fake (despite medical documentation,) and eventually he quit. The owner of the school refused to pay out his holidays, to pay his worked hours, and threatened to contact the Office for Foreigners (*Ausländerbehörde*) to have his visa cancelled. Theoretically this would have meant he would have had to leave Germany almost immediately.

Luckily, though, he had already lawyered up. After some months the school owner settled out of court, paid his holidays out, and was chastised by the court for harassing a foreigner in this manner. It didn't stop her from doing it again one year later, unfairly dismissing another American teacher who also won his case in court.

My purpose here isn't to warn you off English teaching – not at all! Rather, my purpose is to ask you to be careful as a foreign worker, to check the details of your work contracts, and to be aware that there are unscrupulous employers who will seek to play on your visa status, your lack of intimate knowledge of labour laws, and your communication skills (in the local language).

Discrimination can be experienced across race, gender, nationality, and more. Know your rights and obligations, and stand up when they're being infringed upon.

And this is where we move on to diplomacy. Kristen also covered this when she wrote about her relationship with her Serbian boss, how she worked hard, laughed off the small stuff, and yet stood her corner. It's a great point to make, because whenever we travel we are, in small ways, ambassadors for our country.

Think about it – when Bavarians hear that I'm Australian a common reaction is, "drunken Aussies, always starting fights at Oktoberfest." Um, hello? I've never been. And yet the impression exists.

In every interaction we're representing our country. And what better way to contribute positively towards a global impression of our country than to be the diplomat, to shrug off the small stuff, explain the sticky stuff, and celebrate the great stuff.

I love my country, absolutely – Australian big sky shines through my eyes, her sunburnt landscape beats in my heart. She's perfect – not her history (no country's is), not her people (no country's are), but she is. So this love of country and acceptance of flaws are what we carry with us, what we share with the people we meet along our global journey. Conversations are the best way to open eyes and minds, so be prepared to talk, to listen, and to be part of numerous learning journeys – including your own.

Moving On

Jacqueline

When it's time to go home, emotions can be mixed. I remember sitting on an Inter-City Express at Berlin Hauptbahnhof (Central Station), 4 o'clock in the morning, peering out the window bleary-eyed with tiredness and clutching a stale butter pretzel wishing for a Hollywood-style moment where the man of my dreams would step on board and beg me to stay and whisk me away. I didn't want to leave, and yet my visa and bank account spoke otherwise.

And I remember, as a child, sitting impatiently on the plane at Apia Airport (Samoa), willing the engine to start so that we could get back to Australia.

We pack our experiences into our mental bag, stow them safely, and take the next step in our global journey. Sometimes that next step is voluntary, sometimes not. Sometimes it's conscious or dramatic or significant, and sometimes there's a gently drifting away and we find ourselves in new surrounds.

Either way, a new chapter begins.

When abroad, the skill set you need to rely on to cope with change is the same as in your home country, only you've got to add cultural awareness into the mix.

If you're contracted to work somewhere and want to prematurely end that contract, take a look at your conditions before signaling your intentions and ensure you do things by the book. Same goes for rental contracts, should you have signed one. When I wanted to pack it all in here and return home, I didn't realise that I was responsible for finding a tenant to take over the lease on my flat. In Australia, that's the landlord or real estate agent's responsibility.

If you're fired, bite back the snarly retort (unlike me!) and check the conditions of any contract. Is your employer required by law to provide you with a reference or confirmation of employment? Are you entitled to have holidays paid out? Make sure you're familiar with any employer (and employee) obligations while resisting the urge to burn bridges with the person who fired you. I've known two American guys here in Germany who successfully sued their former (German) employer for unpaid leave (see the previous section!)

Kristen

Thanks Jacqui. I had some "high-flying" ideas at age 22 for when my Irish and Scottish work visas would eventually run out. The goal was to then move to London after all was said and done, start working in an art-related job, and possibly apply and be accepted to *The Royal College of Art* for graduate studies. Bonus points if my then German crush at the time (met on a *Green Tortoise* bus trip through Baja, Mexico two years earlier) would move to London as well. It all seemed perfectly reasonable at the time. (Yikes! What was I thinking?)

My glorious plans also hinged on whether or not I could get my second passport from Portugal that I had applied for so that I could legally stay and work within the European Union.

Alas, while I love my people, the Portuguese are not generally known for their bureaucratic speed. My passport and official citizenship (thanks to the fact that my grandparents were born in Portugal) wouldn't be ready for a few more years.

I wanted to stay in Europe but I didn't have the work permission to do so. I suppose even my illegal sketchbook drawings couldn't keep me there.

So I applied to three graduate schools in the most international American city I could think of -New York City! Life had a whole host of adventures lined up for me (not to mention a huge wad of student loans to pay back) that I could never have anticipated earlier. I even met my future (now current) husband in the Big Apple. A German no less!

I suppose my point here is that if you find yourself living and working abroad and then just as suddenly have no choice but to return home again, that might still be OK. The only thing constant in life is change, so learning to embrace change is an all-important life skill.

And after seven short years living back in my home country, I again found myself on a plane moving back to Europe, this time for a university teaching job in Rome, Italy. You just never know what opportunities will come your way. Stay open-minded and embrace those adventures life wants you to have, no matter where they may be.

SOME FINAL KEY POINTS TO REMEMBER

- **Be scrappy, optimistic, flexible and persistent when looking and applying for**

short-term work. Also, hang on to your sense of humor and manage your own expectations.

- **Do your research** on your adopted country before you arrive and always be willing to learn as you go along.

- **Remember that you are an ambassador for your home country.** So please do act accordingly to help educate others and dispel bad stereotypes.

- **But do not take any crap** in the form of discrimination, harassment, blackmail, or anything else unjust of the sort. Learn your rights and get help from sympathetic locals when needed.

- **We're not in Kansas anymore.** Expect differences both minor and major in your host country. Still have that sense of humor? Great! You'll need it.

All right. Are you ready for some more international adventures of the volunteer and internship variety? Just turn the page (or click the pretty button) and let's talk possibilities shall we?

Chapter 3. Volunteer Work and Internships Abroad

"Wherever you turn, you can find someone who needs you. Even if it is a little thing, do something for which there is no pay but the privilege of doing it. Remember, you don't live in the world all of your own."
-Albert Schweitzer

Why Volunteer or Intern Abroad: The Many Benefits

Kristen

Hold on. This is supposed to be a book about *working* abroad. So why on Earth would I start telling you about volunteer and internship opportunities where you don't even get paid?

Well, I have a secret. Back when I was in elementary school I used to dream about helping kids like myself in faraway lands. Influenced in particular by the scenes of starving children in Ethiopia that were on television so often in the 1980s, I didn't understand why on my side of the TV my friends and I were well fed, lived in small houses, and had free public school to attend while on *their* side of the TV it was starvation, suffering, and chaos.

I was also captivated by the images in old *National Geographic* magazines of women in colorful saris washing clothes in the Ganges River in India and the strange-shaped alphabets (Burmese, the language I am currently studying in 2017 among them) featured in my beloved *Children's Book of Knowledge*.

You might have noticed in the previous chapter that my first working abroad stints were in countries that shared my own first language and had relatively similar cultures. That was about all the adventure I could handle at that time in my life as a novice traveler! However by volunteering abroad within a structured and safe environment (through the wonderful *Peace Corps*-esq organization Cross Cultural Solutions) I was able to dip my toes into more exotic worlds and live and work among locals while helping their communities at the same time.

No, I did not get paid for my two month-long work stints teaching and setting up schools in India and Tanzania respectively, but they remain two of the most worthwhile experiences I've had in my entire life. I'll be cherishing those memories someday (hopefully not any time soon) on my deathbed along with many others.

Kristen volunteer teaching in Meyog Village in India. 2000.

Some of the benefits of volunteering and taking internships abroad include:

- **The Ability to Explore.** -Exposure to cultures vastly different from your own.

- **Coming Into Your Own.** -Gaining the confidence that comes from living and working in a country where the language, customs, religions, and norms are vastly different from your own.

- **Full Cultural Immersion.** -The opportunity to live and work among local people and to experience a country and culture more thoroughly than a passing tourist arriving on a guided bus tour ever would.

- **Career Skills.** -The ability to learn and fine-tune skills you can add to your resume and use in your career.

- **University Credits.** -For those of you in university, you can often get college credit for your experiences for roughly the same amount of money you would have paid to take a class on campus.

- **The Bigger Picture.** -Seeing firsthand how lucky you've actually been all your life (especially among people who may never have the opportunity to buy a plane ticket) and how badly needed your own particular and unique talents are in helping others in need.

Have I convinced you yet that *not* being paid to work abroad might actually turn out to be priceless? If so, the next step is to then figure out how we might then fund such an amazing overseas opportunity.

Jacqueline

Thanks, Kristen! Just one more thing to add on this… Another way to volunteer is deciding to take part once you're already settled into the host country you've been living in as a way of giving back, of making a deeper contribution, or of making new contacts, and getting to know new people.

There are so many opportunities to get involved, depending on where you are and where your interests and skills lie.

In 2015, Europe became a new home to more than a million people fleeing war in the Middle East, and poverty in Africa. In my local area, we greeted asylum seekers from a number of lands, predominantly Syria. It was a challenging time on many different levels for the German administration and people, much more so for the families who had experienced such horrors in their home country, horrors leading them to make perilous journeys to unknown lands.

Now, I'm an action person. And I'm a former Girl Guide (similar to a Girl Scout in the US), meaning it's ingrained in me to help people. So I attended the first meeting of locals wanting to help our new neighbours and I became a co-founder of a non-for-profit organization, *Flüchtlingshilfe Plauen e.V.* (Refugees' Help Plauen). Along with another woman, the magnificent Sandra, we rented a small ground floor flat in which we set up a donation centre for clothing and toys. Locals could come and bring their items, which we would sort through and stack on shelves donated by one of my clients. Newly arrived asylum seekers could come to us, some still in the salt-encrusted clothing of their sea journey, and select suitable clothing and items for the kiddies.

Throughout this period, I met amazing locals whose hearts were full of welcome. I spoke to men and women with harrowed eyes, tired from long journeys, and looking into uncertain futures.

And I broke out of my shell and experienced a different side of the town I'd lived in for so many years. This was a different kind of integration, a different kind of experience.

So where volunteering could be your first step to take you abroad, it could also be something you dive into when you're already up and away. Either way, it's something that adds such value to both the travelling experience and also your contribution to the world.

On this topic of volunteering, though, we should hear from Andrea, who's from Pennsylvania, though currently splitting her time between Washington DC and Malawi. Andrea works in international development, helping countries build digital health systems for healthcare workers, and has had her fair share of contact with volunteer groups and programs.

Expat Tales: Andrea Fletcher - American Living 50% of the time in Malawi

> *"When I was 23 I went to Kenya to work on a research study as a graduate student. I ended up living in a village for three months that cares for HIV/AIDs orphans in a remote area. We had*

very poor electricity and little running water. I spent a lot of time in the clinic there trying to better understand what the health data was like.

What I learned was that while the paper health record systems were incredibly poor, everyone seemed to have a cell phone. It was a humbling experience, yet also reminded me a lot of the place where I grew up – another village, just far away. In both places on a Friday evening everyone would be at a football game, one is just American football and eating hot dogs, and the other is playing "futbol" and eating samosas.

Small towns really are not that different in terms of their day-to-day function. This all lead me to a job, post –graduate studies working for a start-up tech firm building cell phone apps for health workers, and moving to Cape Town full time.

I was never the kid that wanted to go on Safari or see the elephants. It was my sister's dream, not mine. I always wanted to go to India, and when I finally did, I realized that I actually belonged back on the African continent. It's become my "nyumbani" or home over the years and I love how different parts of it are, yet how there are similarities between regions and countries. It's a place that is often romanticized or misunderstood, and Africa has really taught me how complex and nuanced the world often is.

I have a lot of opinions on volunteering abroad, mostly because I run into a lot of missionaries and volunteers in sub-Saharan Africa. Really, really, think about if you are doing it to help people or just go on a trip. You might be better off just backpacking and staying in hostels.

Many volunteers are actually a burden because they lack the skill-sets necessary to do meaningful work, and they take away jobs that could have been given to locals. I've heard stories of foreigners building schools etc. and they had to be torn down and rebuilt because they were structurally unsound. A bunch of teenagers who don't have carpentry skills trying to build a building is likely not a good idea.

If you don't speak the language, can't commit to more than a few weeks, and have no experience in what you are doing, it might be better for you to just go on vacation or donate the money from your trip to the organization.

Also, make sure you do your due diligence and research on the organizations. Many are mismanaged, or not capable of handling "volun-tourism."

Work with organizations that know what they're doing and handle these types of trips. It's fine to volunteer on a trip, but make sure that you do your research and that the organization and locals will actually benefit from your time."

FUNDING YOUR EXPERIENCE

Kristen

Back in Chapter 2 I gave a rundown on many tried and true ways to make money before embarking on a short-term work holiday or any longer-term global adventure abroad. All of those tactics will also work for volunteer and unpaid internship abroad stints as well.

Here I'd like to elaborate on a tactic previously mentioned: **Online Crowdfunding**.

Of course many people can and do online Crowdfunding to help finance study abroad experiences, international vacations, and other less altruistic ambitions (like obtaining mass quantities of beer.)

I suggest online Crowdfunding as particularly effective when you are volunteering abroad because people love to change the world by proxy and help contribute to worthwhile causes. Better still, your immediate family and friends in particular will love supporting a travel experience that enriches YOU (gives you the experience of cultural immersion, exposure to new languages, skills, and CV-enhancing opportunities) as well as helping an entire community of people (the people you will be serving as a volunteer or intern) at the very same time.

Now Crowdfunding is tricky and much harder than it looks. Don't get me wrong, if done *correctly*, Crowdfunding can be the ace up your sleeve that you need to pull off making your dreams of international work abroad a reality!

Unfortunately, most people think that if they spend five minutes setting up a "give me money" page at *Indiegogo.com*, *Gofundme.com*, or others that they just need to hit "publish" and the dollars will start rolling in. It just does *not* work that way. (I have over thirteen years of experience raising money online for worthy causes and have raised over $125,000 through my website http://aurashouse.com so far in case you were wondering where my sentiments come from.)

Too many people cobble together a poorly thought-out and badly-worded/crafted project and then try to launch it all in the same day as some kind of afterthought on their to-do list. The goals are usually way too high ($10K when really a first-time crowdfunder should stick to goals of $1K or under to start, for example).

Most "failed" or "failing" Crowdfunding campaigns start off with a random story about the person doing the fundraising instead of the beneficiary and why they should be given assistance. In essence the text fails to inspire the potential donor and show them how *they can become the hero of this story* and make something wrong in this world into a big right.

With the actual project flawed or just weak and uninspiring, the crowdfunder then launches it, does one (maybe two) mass social media postings and then sits there and wonders why the donations do not come rolling in.

There is a better way. It is simple and yet it's hard because it means leaving your comfort zone.

The magic and simple formula (boiled down in a nutshell) for Crowdfunding success is this:

1.) **Start with yourself.** The first donation needs to come from YOU. If you don't care about your own project, no one else will. You can make one $50 donation to get things rolling or donate $20 as yourself and the rest in smaller amounts as "anonymous" or in loving memory of someone you love. This gets your number of supporters up as well as showing everyone who visits your page that you have raised more than a big fat zero. (*Nobody* wants to donate to a project that has raised $0.) If you only have $5, then just *donate* $5. If you don't care enough about your own project to donate even a little bit to it then you will most likely *not* be successful.

2.) **Next, you need to get your family and friends on board.** Ask them via well-crafted *individual* **personalized emails or messages** that address them by name. It doesn't matter how much they donate at this point, only that they are slowly raising the donation amount *and* being counted as a supporter. Never underestimate the power of "social proof" during the first day, week, and month of your campaign. The more people you can list helping you, the better for you and your cause.

3.) **Acquaintances and more distant contacts come next.** If they see a decent number of people already supporting your project as well as the amount raised going up (no matter how slowly) they will be more likely to donate and support your cause.

4.) **Finally, complete strangers may start to support your cause, usually after you've gotten at least 60% of the way to your goal.** You may even snag a much-coveted "hero donor." These are the ones who will finish the entire project off if you are close enough to your goal, knowing that they were the ones to make this Crowdfunding dream come true for you, for your recipient, and for all your supporters.

5.) **Rinse and repeat.** Did the donations stall or stop coming in? Donate again yourself! Send out an update. Be creative and come up with a raffle, incentive, or fundraising event offline to help boost online totals. Make an announcement at work or school and put out a collection jar. Show up! (Sorry. I've seen too many Crowdfunding projects sitting online collecting dust with no one steering the ship.)

The important thing again to reignite momentum is not to get discouraged. Even adding $1 to your total now and then keeps your project alive and moving in the right direction. If it takes months, then so be it. If you need to think of your project as a bank account that you can only make a small deposit into each week, then so be it. Slow and steady wins the race.

These tips, incidentally also apply to starting a new Facebook group, launching an online course, putting up an eBook, or starting a business. The formula is exactly the same. 1.) Start with yourself. 2.) Get the support of your family and friends next (social proof). 3.) Reach out to acquaintances and strangers last. 4.) Rinse and repeat.

If you are serious about using the power of Crowdfunding to help fund your volunteer or internship abroad experience I invite you to have a look at my easy-to-use book *Crowdfunding Confidential: Raise Money For You and Your Cause*. There I can give you more details on planning, creating, and launching your first successful Crowdfunding campaign and have you up and running in about one hour.

Staff and students at Maua Hills Training Centre where Kristen taught in 2005 - Eve, Hope, and Pauline (Moshi, Tanzania.)

VOLUNTEERING ABROAD, INTERNSHIPS, AND STUDYING ABROAD: KNOW BEFORE YOU GO

Kristen

There are many ways to choose a volunteer, study abroad, or internship experience. Obviously if you are a student looking to get university credit for your work abroad you should be choosing which program you sign up for based on your major or area of study, interests, and your capacity to best help out. You also need to ensure that the program you are signing up for will be accepted by your university and that they will award you credit for your work.

I have acted as an Academic Advisor to university students since 2000 including for those who went abroad to a foreign university for a semester or two as well as those who were adding internships to their program sheets.

My biggest piece of advice would be to always communicate with your Academic Advisor and university program sooner rather than later. Better still, if you are a Freshman or Sophomore (1st or 2nd year university student for those of you outside the US) planning to study abroad in your Junior (3rd) year you should already bring up your intentions to your advisor even if it seems way too early.

The Fall semester of your Junior (3rd) year is by far the most popular time to study or intern abroad though it can also be done a tad later. Most advisors, myself included, would recommend you are back at home at least for your final university semester to tie up loose ends and attend that graduation ceremony.

Now, some advisors are better than others (I consider myself the best of the best, modesty aside) so a good one will begin planning your program sheet to allow for the "disruption" a semester or two abroad or internship experience might bring.

They will insist you get your required and lower level courses out of the way first to then make room for "free electives" where your study abroad/ internship credits most likely will come in. They will also help you do your research on the best schools and programs for your unique situation or point you to the Study Abroad Office where you can look into your options with help and guidance from trained staff or faculty standing by.

As for internships, if your university has a Career and/or Internship Office you should be knocking on their door as soon as possible. (I recommend doing this anyway even if you aren't planning on studying or working abroad.)

Most students expect that the Career/Internship Office will find and arrange internships for them. This is sometimes the case, but the vast majority of students must find their own internships.

Make sure that whichever position you are considering or chosen for is kosher with your university, Academic Advisor, and Career/Internship Office before signing the dotted line and buying your plane tickets.

You'll need to find out how many credits you will be awarded and how they will come into your academic program sheet. For example, if you get three credits for a three-month internship and it comes in as a Free Elective on your program sheet, don't be complaining that there's no room later to take "Underwater Basket Weaving 101" or whichever free course looks enticing to you.

Free Electives are meant to give you some freedom in what you choose to study away from your major (in the American university system anyway) so consider first if using one for an internship is in your best interests. (It usually is.) You may also find that if your internship is closely enough related to your major area of study, those credits come in as an upper level elective for your major instead.

Many students often also do an internship first, usually over the summer, and wonder if they can get credit for it later. It's always better to get permission first from your university, but if you find yourself in this situation it doesn't hurt to ask your Academic Advisor if you can still obtain credits.

At *The American University of Rome* our policy traditionally has been that students can do an internship in advance but then must enroll in a 3 credit Internship course in the Fall or Spring semester to check in with the Internship Advisor and present their findings and experiences to the other internship students via final presentations. Each university has different rules so communication is key!

You know what they say about people who *assume* things (They make an "ass out of u and me" ...), so do your research, plan accordingly, work hard, and smugness is sure to follow.

MORE ABOUT THE BENEFITS OF INTERNSHIPS

How do I love internships? Let me count the ways! First off, they are proven to be the most effective way to get a career-enhancing job later on -more important than your grades, extracurricular activities, or which frat or sorority house you belonged to.

I've worked with many students over the years who did internships who learned new skills that helped them get hired full time later as well as those who *hated* their internship experiences so much, they went into opposite career directions entirely.

I was one of the latter kids. Warning: flashback crossing ahead! (Insert mid 90s music playlist here.)

You remember I was studying painting back in the day yes? Well, I loved (and still love) painting. But I had it in my head back then as an idealistic sort that art could change the world. I believed that people could be moved to think and act more altruistically to their fellow human beings through the transformative power of images. Positive social change *could* be achieved with just the right color here and brushstroke there.

But what sorts of jobs do people who study painting actually get? The career office at my school pointed me in the direction of becoming an "art gallery attendant."

So on one slushy early spring day in Boston in my 19th year of life, I got an online list of all the art galleries in Provincetown, Massachusetts. P-Town as we also affectionately call it, was America's very first art colony.

It is home to an eccentric and lively crowd (read: it's a haven for the LGBT community, artists, writers, nut-jobs, grizzled old Portuguese sea-farers, and wide-eyed dreamers) and is where many New York and Boston artists go "to summer." Who knew "summer" could also be a verb? Ah the benefits of an internship!

So I composed a letter to each gallery owner, included my resume, sealed the envelopes, licked those stamps, posted about thirty-something letters explaining why I was *the* perfect future intern and waited with bated breath for an avalanche of answers.

I received one reply. It was from a gallery then known as *Gallery 299* on Commercial St. In a nutshell Brian, the owner said, "Sure. Come meet me in a few weeks and start as a paid (score!) intern." *Note: I had to change all the names here. You'll learn why in a moment.

So I arranged to get academic credit for my summer work with Mass Art's career office. I booked a summer cottage (aka: run down old shack behind an Italian restaurant in Wellfleet, MA.) with my high-school sweetheart (a very bad move it turned out as we were already on the rocks,) and packed my trunk for a summer on the whimsical tip of Cape Cod.

What I learned that summer was that art in a Provincetown gallery, at least in this particular gallery, was not for enlightening the masses. It was destined to be procured by the wealthy and hung in their living rooms where their rich friends might also see it during dinner parties and the like. These art-lovers did not buy a painting because it spoke to them. Rather they bought because "Robert So and So *is so hot* right now!" These were investments in fact and nothing to get sentimental about.

I often would sit in the empty gallery staring at the parade of tourists and locals walking to and fro along Commercial Street. Alone with the art, I would send out invitations to gallery openings to first "The A List" and then "The B and C Lists" as per Brian's request.

The gallery's owner himself was a large, redheaded 6.5-foot husky giant of around age 30. He was dating his "star artist" (a very talented guy whom I still follow and admire) and came from a privileged family in Connecticut whom he implied were not thrilled with his lifestyle "choice."

I learned this summer and the following summer (yes, I went back) that in fact, the gallery-sitting life was *not* for me. So even though I got to hang my own art there as a little workplace perk, I learned what I did *not* want to do with my life. I didn't want to sell or make art that would hang in some wealthy broker's living room largely unseen and unloved.

How did it all end up? Well, I got a small salary and six academic elective credits over two summers, I got to participate in art shows in P-town (great for my CV), and I made a ton of new friends and memories. One of the most unforgettable moments was the day my boss Brian, disappeared abruptly in the middle of the night leaving both the gallery's landlord and myself unpaid and scratching our heads. (It was a bonding moment for us. My husband and I often pop in to say hi even to this day when we come visit P-Town.)

We learned later that Brian had fled to China after failing miserably to pay the commission money due to his angry artists as well as his rent, and … the world's best intern! I'm sure he'd have some expat stories to share with you here but he's too busy "blending in" somewhere in Beijing perhaps.

Note: Jacqui and I don't recommend you use this book to run from the law by skipping town and hiding out abroad!

So let's hear now from a more recent intern who actually *did* like their placement. Take it away Kendra!

Expat Tales: Kendra Hunter -American who lived in Italy, now back in the USA

> *"I moved abroad to Rome, Italy in the fall of 2014, to finish my Bachelor's degree at The American University of Rome. Even though a lot of people didn't agree with me moving overseas as a single mother with a 3 year-old, I decided to set out on this adventure anyway. I told myself if I could find*

a place to live and childcare for my daughter, I was going to do it.

I was a little bit delusional before we moved however. I thought I could afford to pay to rent a room in a flat I found on Craigslist for 650 euros a month. I also thought that I would somehow have enough to pay a nanny 10 euros an hour to watch my daughter while I attended classes. Luckily what I planned out isn't what happened.

Although we did stay in the flat I found on Craigslist for about a month... it didn't work out, and neither did the nanny. I was fortunate enough to meet my best friend Nina, at AUR. She helped me enroll my daughter in an Italian school and helped me find our new flat both of which were much better priced than our first options. My mom always joked that I'm like a cat that always lands on its feet, and thanks to Nina we were able to land right back on our feet.

Once I was settled into college life abroad I took on two internships or "volunteerships" depending who you ask. The first was at the Food and Agricultural Organization of the United Nations where I worked on a program called RuralInvest that teaches rural communities how to build a sustainable business. My main job was creating and translating a software user manual for RuralInvest.

The second was with LoveItaly!, a non-profit organization that is dedicated to the preservation, promotion, and appreciation of Italian cultural heritage. While working with LoveItaly! I helped organize a charity gala to support the efforts to preserve a Domus in Pompeii. I focused mainly on gathering cash and prize donations from local businesses.

Both of these internships I got through the internship program through my university. Although I wasn't sure I was qualified to perform the job functions required, due to my lack of Italian language skills, I managed to successfully complete both of my internship programs.

I found out that surviving life abroad is like getting a good job. It's about who you know. I never would've survived Italy without the friends I made, and I never would have had the opportunities to work at FAO and LoveItaly! had it not been for my professor at AUR arranging everything.

Networking with other expats and locals when living abroad is a must. Not only can they provide useful advice, but they also offer a level of understanding that your friends and family back home can't provide."

Kendra mentioned that she couldn't have succeeded as an intern without the support of her wonderful internship advisor. Let's hear now from my fabulous former colleague Kathleen at The American University of Rome who helped Kendra and hundreds of other lucky students get those crucial first work experiences in Rome and beyond.

Expat Tales: Professor Kathleen Fitzsimmons - American teaching at The American University of Rome in Italy

> *"An internship is often a life-altering experience. In my 10 years of placing students and overseeing their internships, I've had cases of students who have discovered talents they didn't know they had, interest in industries or sectors they hadn't known before, and passions ignited by great managers and good products.*

> *I had one student who, on the flip side, discovered she hated the business (hotel management) she interned in, and was happy to have saved herself the agony of learning that lesson after graduation!*

> *Internships give students the ability to add "I can's" and "I know how's" to their CVs. I can write a marketing plan, design a webpage, write an effective tweet, edit a film, build a database, do a telephone market research campaign, or create a grant proposal. These are all "I can's" that some of my former interns cited in their exit presentations.*

*They overcame fears, took risks, explored new
areas of interest, and built confidence. An
internship is a safe opportunity for students to take
risks and investigate functions or businesses in
which they might want to work.*

*Adding that critical real-world experience to a CV
is more important today than ever, as the data
from employers tells us that work experience is the
single most important factor they look at when
hiring - more important than the school the student
went to or her grades or her extracurricular
activities."*

VOLUNTEERING BEFORE FINDING PAID WORK

Kristen

OK. We covered short-term volunteer work
placements as well as how to get academic credit and
the possibility of a stipend or salary by becoming an
intern abroad.

But what if you have already landed in your new
country and are not having any luck finding traditional
work at the start?

One possible solution is you begin meeting new
people, networking, and gaining more work leads by
volunteering.

Some of my favorite places to find volunteer (and job) opportunities by country are at *Idealist.org* as well as through *Craigslist*. But you might also find organizations, institutions, and companies that interest you and contact them directly to see if they are hiring or looking for volunteers.

Your volunteer gig might also be something you do on the side if you are fortunate enough to already have found paid employment. Use your volunteer experience to meet new people, acquire new skills, to show off your expertise, and learn more about the place or industry you really do want to work in.

Let's hear from Valerie to see how her volunteer work stints helped lead to full time employment later on.

Expat Tales: Valerie -Brazilian who lived in the USA, Australia, Switzerland, and France

> *"Several years after working in the USA, I moved to Australia. After taking a few courses in different schools I got two volunteer jobs in order to start off my CV in Australia. Then I had a couple of temporary jobs. The last was just for a week at the Alexander International College. They liked my work so much that I ended up staying for three months with a full salary. I was very proud of myself.*

After that I was hired at an Accountant's office. I had to do a few specific courses. I had a good salary, but one of the owners turned out to be a very bad person and after a few months I was dismissed.

In Switzerland I was very lucky. I went for an interview for a secretary position and... I got the job! It was very audacious since it was also my very first job in French, which was not my mother tongue and I did not know much at the time. Well, it was a good start for my Swiss CV, but after three months I had to leave the job because my boss was sexually harassing me. Again the good wind was blowing in my direction and four days later I was hired in a place where I was going to stay for ten years. I loved my job and I had a very good position as a commercial and administrative assistant."

MAXIMIZE YOUR EXPERIENCE: AFTER YOUR STINT ENDS

Kristen

Now I know you took that volunteer position or unpaid internship for the purest of altruistic reasons, but the fact of the matter is that you can now add the experience to your resume or CV and use it to shine when a prospective employer reads it.

Allow your time helping orphans in Kolkata, India to help you start a conversation with your interviewer on your passion for helping children at that pre-school you are now applying for. Or if you are looking to get your foot in the door at a new tech start up, share how you helped raise money for a computer lab at the Vocational Training Center you volunteered at in Ghana.

Yes, you helped a lot of people during your time as a volunteer or intern, but what goes around comes around. So take a bow and let that experience continue to help you move forward as you start looking for paid work as well.

SOME FINAL KEY POINTS TO REMEMBER

- **Volunteer to help others and also to gain new skills for yourself.** Choose to serve in a country you are dying to learn about and explore. Choose industries where you already have some background or interest or go in the opposite direction to begin acquiring new skills, but only if the organization you will be working for states clearly that they will be training. Volunteer to be of service, not to become a burden.

- **Don't burn bridges.** Remember, you are there to help, not be catered to. Having a great "can-do," optimistic, self-starting attitude will go a long way and get you noticed at your volunteer placement. You may not be getting paid, but this experience may very well help you get a paying job later on. Don't forget the people you are working with today could be valuable references later on.

- **East or west, internships are the best.** If you are currently a student, *strongly* consider signing up for an internship before you graduate. The positive effect the right (or wrong) internship could have on your future career is immeasurable.

- **Internships can also be for those looking to make a career change.** No longer a student? No problem. As Robert DeNiro recently illustrated in the Hollywood film, *The Intern,* internships can be for anyone no matter your age. Just come with a good attitude and a willingness to learn and reap the rewards.

- **But don't allow yourself to be exploited!** Volunteer experiences and unpaid internships can also be a front for unscrupulous and cheap employers looking to get free labor without providing training or anything in return. For this reason, only sign on with reputable organizations or get expert advice from career counselors, trusted mentors, and others who have your back.

And here's one last bit of advice from Andrea Fletcher, our American expat working 50% of the time in sub-Saharan Africa as the Lead Data Strategist for Cooper Smith:

> *"Be humble. Commit to a good length of time. Have low expectations on what you can accomplish as an intern in a foreign country."*

On this last point we have to agree. Time appears to run slower in some countries and it may even be hard to see where you made progress at the end of your stint. Take heart! No act of kindness is ever wasted and every experience you have is useful for your own personal growth.

So what if you are still not ready to go back home? Let's have a look at some longer-term work opportunities in the next chapter!

CHAPTER 4: LONG-TERM WORK AND CAREERS ABROAD

*The loneliness of the expatriate is of an odd
and complicated kind, for it is inseparable from
the feeling of being free, of having escaped.*
–Adam Gopnik

Kristen

Not long ago I taught my first "in-person" course at a
marketing, public relations, and media production firm
known as Mango Group here in Yangon.

After living in Myanmar for several months and
despite arriving as a virtual blank slate with no special
connections, leads, or anything, I've managed to
somehow find ways to put my unique skills and
talents to work to both pay the bills as well as to
contribute and be of service in my new host country.

I fortunately have many "pots on the fire" including my
online teaching on various digital platforms, helping to
set up the new American University of Myanmar,
freelance and consulting gigs that come and go with
the wind, and now this new stint teaching creative
professionals office and intercultural communication,
productivity, and better creative workflow practices at
Mango Group.

And though my inner feminist cringes, I would be remiss not to mention that for those of you who are hitched or "partnered-up" it is especially helpful if your other half has some kind of job or business as well, helping to ensure you can both eat every day. It all fits into the mix.

I bring all this up because it illustrates perfectly the ingredients you will need to successfully work abroad for both short and long term stints.

You will need

- **Heaps of flexibility**
  -So you can match your unique skills and past experiences to people, places, companies, and situations you never might have considered or knew existed back in your home country.

  (A friend of mine just *thinking* about attending medical school was put to work on Day 1 helping to deliver babies in a rural clinic in Tanzania when we were volunteering there in 2005. Never underestimate the value of your education and skills particularly in places where you are needed the most! My friend is a doctor now and occasionally goes back to Africa to deliver babies and help out in rural clinics when she can. Full circle!)

- **A generous helping of audacity**
  Who are you to take the lead, teach a team, or head a local organization in such a far-flung

place? You might not feel 100% qualified for the opportunities that come looking for you but the big secret is virtually no one is 100% qualified to do anything! You need to rely on what you already know, commit to researching and learning what you don't know, and having the courage to step out of your comfort zone and just go for it. This applies in any country, but especially in developing countries where your skills may especially be in demand.

- **A pinch of resignation**
  The job you are looking at doesn't match the daydream you had in your head? You have much control over what jobs you seek and apply for but you may find that situations and events have a mind of their own. Be open to all the possibilities even if they seem out there at first.

- **An ample sense of humor**
  That's pretty much the only thing that got me through my birdfeeder factory job right out of school and those first few weeks as a dazed "trailing spouse" (I hate that term!) after our recent move to Myanmar.

  You are a clown. -A fumbling foreign buffoon trying to make your way in a strange land. So what! You are also a clown who gets to live and work abroad, living a life of your own design. "Nya nya nya nya nyaaaa!"

Kristen (third from top left) with students at The American University of Rome. 2014.

Finding Your Ideal Long-Term Job

Jacqueline

One thing which can be said about Generation X (of which I'm a proud member), or the alphabetized "Generations" which follow, is that we're not as tied to our jobs as our Baby Boomer parents' generation. Whereas in the past there was an education, a job, a 45-year career path in one firm and then retirement, today we are flexible, footloose, fancy-free… for the most part.

Many of us consider changing jobs a regular occurrence, or if not, then certainly not something unusual. We seek out our own opportunities, grab them by the horns, and shake our careers into submission. Some of us can also limp from one unsatisfying job to another, but the thinking is the same: onwards and upwards, the working world is mine to make of as I will. Okay, okay, that is likely me projecting, but have a think about it – would *you* seriously consider staying with the one firm for your entire career? Ah, I thought not.

And so we now move on to this idea of a long-term job abroad. No more volunteering, no more internships, no more wondering what the next week or month will bring. No, now we're getting serious! We're starting to put down some roots.

Let's look at a few different scenarios here for finding that ideal long-term job. There are traditional routes, such as job advertisements on LinkedIn, Monster, Seek and so on which are easy enough to apply for though it can be difficult to stand out from the crowd in an ever-increasing moveable feast of a global workforce. But it's certainly worth a shot.

Often it can be a case of not what you know, but rather *who* you know. In these situations it can also be possible to find work through your new network of international friends, made via expatriate groups such as *InterNations*.

Then there's the scenario where a combination of luck and hard *yakka* (an Australian term for "hard work") pay off. This was my experience – I came for a holiday, stayed longer for a job I literally stumbled into, and it's become my career, my calling. Additionally, it's been a job that I have been able to shape to fit my skills, experiences, strengths, and weaknesses.

If you're not moving abroad with a specific job offer, as my friend Cate recently did upon her return to London, it could be you follow a path similar to Brie, who started abroad as an English trainer (something we look more closely at in a moment) and then, after learning the local language and integrating into the local culture, find a job better suited to your skill set, experience, education, and interests.

Taking the Brie example, your pathway to success depends primarily on your chutzpah and on playing the long game. If you're in it for the long haul, you'll be patient in going through the early work phases (as described in previous chapters), you'll keep your eye on the market, and when the time is right you'll find that job, apply, be interviewed, and get started.

The main point I want to make here is to be patient. When working abroad and looking for that long-term job, you're competing with applicants from the local market. My top tips?

- **Do your research:** learn about the local market.

- **Translate any qualifications on your CV or resume** (and pay the extra money to have them done by a professional – this will likely require having the translation signed and stamped.)

- **Check that your qualifications are recognized in your new home country.**

Ensure your CV meets local standards: what is customary to include in your country of origin may not be customary in your new home (for example, German CVs commonly include the applicant's photo and personal information such as gender and marital status. These are all no-nos in Australia.)

On this point, Max has a few things to say, so I'll hand over to him.

Expat Tales: Max Amolloh -Kenyan living in Australia

"I'm originally from a small village in Kenya, and now I do two jobs. First, I'm working as a disability support worker. My background is in Human Services and I work for a not-for-profit organization as a social support officer looking after programs for people who are infected by HIV and viral hepatitis.

Before I came to Australia, my then fiancé had sent me a catalogue of youth apprentice jobs available and had asked me to look and decide what I wanted to do. After looking again and again, I told myself that I wanted to become a mechanic. I was convinced, not because I had any experience, but because I was imagining salary, long-term employment, and the demand for those skills. By the way, I was so excited about this prospect that I thought this job was waiting for me on arrival.

When I landed in Australia I noticed that other than the introduction which is normally your name and where I'm from originally, the toughest question for me was when I got asked what do I do. Because I had made myself an imaginary career, whenever I was asked what I did I would say I'm planning to be a mechanic and that would leave me feeling relaxed and proud.

Anyway, my first job was cleaning in the school where my wife was teaching staff. I got this job because when I went to meet my wife's colleagues, one lady was very excited and after our introduction, I was expecting to be asked, "What do you do?" Instead she asked me, "Do you have a job? " Of course I was jobless and said no. She told me that their school had an employment program for migrants. She then asked me if I was interested in working in the cleaning department.

Judging by standards and the salary a cleaner gets in Kenya, this wasn't a glamorous option, *but me being a quick leaner I noticed that all the cleaners at the school drove to work in their own cars. In Kenya cleaners get one hundred dollars per month. Here I was getting paid $25 (AUD) per hour and I was working 30 hours per fortnight.*

I would recommend that people travelling to new countries, especially those travelling to first world countries, when you want to get a job and you only have qualifications from your country of origin, number one don't expect to be employed at the same level you worked at before moving to the foreign country.

Second, don't be fussy and instead get any job that will give you income because this way, you get to engage with the society more when you do those odd jobs.

Humble yourself because what I found here in Australia is that everyone is equal and there's no perception of superiority like in Kenya."

Thanks, Max.

One point which he touched on which I just wanted to highlight is the importance of networking. To point out the expression again, "it's not what you know but who you know," and we see this in Max's experience of finding his first job in his new country.

In my line of work, many of my clients came via word-of-mouth (I don't advertise, only have a website.) Some may scoff at the continued power of networking, but it is alive and well and helping people find jobs all over the world.

I'll now hand you over to Kathleen, so she can share her advice:

Expat Advice: Professor Kathleen Fitzsimmons – American Teaching at The American University of Rome, Italy

"In preparing for the leap into the world of work, I suggest that job-seekers become commando networkers.

Not only will they hone their interview skills before having to do actual job interviews, they will learn about different jobs and industries, and build their network of contacts.

When you network you are not asking for a job. You are asking for 20 minutes of someone's time. That someone will most likely be a contact that you or a professor or a parent knows.

Most people when asked for 20 minutes of their time to talk about their job, career, industry, by an earnest and well-prepared student, recent graduate or bright-eyed job-seeker will say yes.

People love to talk about themselves. A good networking interview gets them to do just that.

Make a list of possible contacts. Create 4-5 good open-ended questions to ask - What was your first job and how did it lead to where you are today? What are the leading trends in your industry/sector? What skills/qualities do successful candidates bring to entry-level jobs in your company? What advice would you have for newly minted college grads today?

The approach is low-pressure because you are not actually asking for a job. You are simply asking for time. -And only a little of that.

The objective of such an interview is to get two more names - someone impressed with you or your questions might suggest you talk to two of her colleagues (Do you know of anyone else who might be good for me to talk with?), and so on.

You will follow up, of course, with nice thank you notes via email, and sooner or later, someone might say "So and so is looking for a [fill in the blank] junior product manager, assistant, copywriter, intern, management trainee, social media maven...) and then you can apply, using the name of the contact who suggested it.

It is a fabulous process and a good investment of your time. You will hone your interview skills (because the people you interview will likely ask you about your own experience), get tips for job hunting, learn about a lot of different businesses, and build your network. "

Sage advice. Thanks Kathleen! Let's move on now to a topic near and dear to my heart: teaching abroad.

TEACHING ABROAD

Jacqueline

Teaching abroad can be broken down into a number of categories: teaching English (so, the TESOL we all know about), and teaching in schools abroad (much as my friend Melissa and her husband Clint have been doing for the past decade). Let's first look at teaching English, my bailiwick.

By now you'll be well aware that I'm a language and business skills trainer. And one thing I am passionate about is providing professional, customized services to my clients – this means that all my teachers must be qualified, they must have experience living abroad, and they must have a business background. After all, there's no sense teaching a business manager about business unless you've been there yourself.

What I'm getting at is that teaching abroad is not, in my eyes, an option for a gap year or a whim.

Teaching English is a popular way to get abroad, so definitely worth looking into. A few caveats, though:

- **Get qualified!** By this, I mean make sure you have an internationally recognised TESOL certificate from a reputable institution. These can be undertaken online or in your hometown. People like me, who have opportunities for trainers, won't take a second look if there isn't that qualification. As I always say (and as you see in my book on this topic –Teaching English: Your Guide to Launching a Successful ESL Teaching Career) just because you speak a language, doesn't mean you can teach it!

- **Do your research:** websites such as ESL-Base are not only resource-rich, but also host a pretty handy job board. TeachAway might also be useful for you.

- **Talk to me!** Okay, I'm not here to plug my Facebook group, but I have a steadily growing group of ESL teachers where we share experiences, tips, resources, and more. Join in the conversation!

Now let's look at teaching at schools abroad. I mentioned my friend Melissa. She and her husband have taught in Tanzania, Vietnam, and Japan, and are now located in China. With three kids, it's an adventure for everyone. If you've got a teaching degree then it's worth looking into the options that are available to you. Websites such as <u>TES</u> and <u>eTeach International</u> are good starting points.

The final point I'd like to make about teaching abroad, and this harks back to a point Andrea made earlier about volunteering abroad, is that if you're only in a place for a short time then I don't recommend it. You'd be doing your students a huge disservice to only be in town for a few weeks. Students – regardless of age – invest not only time and money into language training, but also emotion. Teachers and students forge a bond, build a safe space where mistakes can be made and not judged. If you're in town for a while, then make language teaching your thing and be proud you're making a difference in people's lives and opportunities.

And if you're teaching in schools, a time commitment is even more critical.

Alright, so let's keep this concept of making a difference in mind, and let's talk about another great way to serve others while also seeing the world.

HUMANITARIAN WORK

Kristen

One thing I wish I had known about at a younger age was how to build a career as a professional "people helper" abroad. Partaking in humanitarian work is one of the most worthwhile ways to spend a few months, years, or an entire lifetime.

I was always a fan of the UN, especially its *World Food Programme,* the people helping out and feeding those affected by famine, natural disasters, or systemic poverty around the world. They were in fact, the ones on TV handing out rations to those Ethiopian kids I empathized so strongly with back in the 80s.

Little did I know then that I'd later do video and graphic design contract work for the *World Food Programme* as well as convince my future husband to go and submit his resume to them.

Let's hear from my better, more-humanitarian half now!

Expat Tales: Michael Hemling –German who lived in the USA, Italy, now living in Myanmar

"All my life I have been a child of travel. Having a German father and a Russian mother, there was a lot of back and forth between Germany and Russia.

I grew up bilingual and soon learned to appreciate the complexity of this planet. Languages became my passion and I later added English and French to my tool belt. My desire to explore the world had been born and this desire was nourished during my childhood by traveling through virtually every country in Eastern Europe. But I knew that there were limitations. Due to the wall the rest of the world was off limits for me.

That changed in 1989. I was a front row witness to the wall coming down in Berlin and with that came a new world of opportunities.

Once you are out of school, your resume looks quite empty. I was not afraid of work and worked hard to get more experience. At one point, I had three part-time jobs at the same time, on top of a full curriculum at the university. But what I wanted was a big time opportunity somewhere in the world.

That opportunity came knocking in 1994 with an internship in New York City at a Swiss logistics company. I took a year off from my university studies, which was uncommon back then as everybody was rushing through their studies to start their work life.

As an intern I took any opportunity possible, -no job was too difficult and I aimed to show my value to the organization. -And the hard work paid off! In 1997 I was on a flight to New York two days after my last university exam to start my job at the same Swiss logistics company who hired me right after graduation.

In my first year at the job I tried to build my reputation and traveled almost every week between the 45 offices of the organization. What followed were ten amazing years in the United States and the opportunity to expand on my finance, logistics, and accounting skills.

After I met my amazing wife Kristen in New York, the course of my life changed. Kristen and I wanted something different with the possibility to build a family. I followed Kristen to Rome, Italy and plunged myself into a three-month consultancy with the World Food Programme. It was a gamble but I was confident the same hard work ethic I applied in the US would make me successful in Rome. One and a half years later and thanks to my team, the World Food Programme became the first organization in the UN to present its financial statements using International Public Sector Accounting Standards (IPSAS.) I was then offered a year contract and afterwards, a rare opportunity to be hired as a full staff member.

Even though the World Food Programme is the largest humanitarian logistics organization in the world and I was familiar with the mechanics, something was different. It was not anymore about maximizing profits for a company but it was about helping people in need.

WFP has an amazing bond amongst its staff. It is a culture of fast paced responses to challenges and innovative solutions to help millions around the world. If you want to achieve results fast, you are at the right place. Here we focus on achieving results fast for the people we serve. We rely on showing our donors that the food and cash reaches the hands of the beneficiaries as soon as they need it.

Fast forward and I am now writing this essay from Yangon, Myanmar, where I am heading the finance and administration department for the World Food Programme. I am on the frontlines to help assist the people of Myanmar. Nothing is more rewarding than to see the smile on a person's face when they receive the food. At this moment you realize: it takes all people in an organization working hard together to achieve amazing results.

Just a few weeks ago, the World Food Programme became the first humanitarian organization in Myanmar to transfer monetary assistance for buying food rations through mobile phones. The World Food Programme is becoming more and more innovative in the delivery of its assistance. It is a fast paced world we are living in with a huge amount of challenges, but I am up for it to do my part in improving the lives of the people of Myanmar."

Thanks Michael! I hope you also noticed the role a

humble internship had on Michael's future career path.

Now I'd like to introduce you to my former colleague at The American University of Rome and also former student. (She took my Web Design 1 summer class many moons ago!)

Charlotta has some great advice for getting started with the UN as well as other non-profit organizations and can give you a glimpse into the life of doing humanitarian work on a contract/consultancy basis.

Expat Tales: Charlotta Jull –Canadian Who Lives in Italy

"Although I'd say there is no real set path to a UN career, there are a few skills that will make a big difference.

Having a solid command of at least two UN official languages, international development project experience, and a masters-level degree in a related field are often considered basic prerequisites.

In addition, one needs to be very flexible and adaptable to take on assignments of varying length in what some might consider 'hardship' postings. A long-term UN starting position in a North American or European capital is highly unlikely. You may have to accept a lot of unstable, short-term contracts and be willing to uproot on short notice.

Volunteer opportunities with NGOs working on the ground can often be a good stepping-stone towards a first contract with the UN, and offer a more hands-on experience in managing projects than work in a large, hierarchical UN agency.

For those under 30 from participating countries, the Junior Professional Programme (JPO) is also a very good entry point, as it allows for a two-year career-building experience in a UN agency, but it is very competitive, and it does not necessarily lead to long-term opportunities at the higher levels.

Check the list of under-represented countries at the agency you wish to apply for as that will also be a major factor for hiring. Agencies are looking to diversify their applicant pools and often target applicants from the countries they are most involved in assisting.

At the start of my first UN project as an international legal consultant at FAO, I worked alongside a very senior manager who advised me to get as broad an experience as possible and seek out opportunities with other NGOs, and partner agencies in the public as well as private sector in many different countries.

He explained that it is very difficult to enter the UN as a mid-career professional at headquarters. Most either get their start through the JPO programme or are laterally hired for management positions from other organizations.

I would agree that you can build a better skill set from field work than seeking a UN position at headquarters.

My own experience is a combination of determination, luck and also, I would have to admit, a bit of delusion because it is just not easy to do the kind of work that I have been doing with small children, and I've had to pass up a lot of better opportunities for dead-end short-term consultancies lately."

So for those of you thinking of a short or long-term career in the UN, the six official UN working languages currently are: Arabic, Chinese, English, French, Russian, and Spanish.

If you are fluent in English and have at least studied one or more of those other languages, then you can consider applying. The better your language skills though, the better your chances of success!

I do have an American friend who now happily works for the UN who only had a foggy recollection of high school French when she applied. (She's fluent in Italian, but alas, that is not a UN language.) She of course, brushed up on her French skills like mad before the job interview and I'd suggest you do the same, at the very least!

Meanwhile, as I try and get my kids not to lose their Italian they picked up in Rome while they currently tackle Burmese at their new school in Yangon, let's talk more about the importance of language in your new host country and in the workplace.

Jacqui?

HOW IMPORTANT IS LANGUAGE?

Jacqueline

There are varying schools of thought on the importance of language. Can you find work in a country without the local language? Yes. Do I recommend it? No. Can you integrate with your new neighbours without the local language? No.

My first three years in Germany were spent in a whirlwind of teaching (40 contact hours a week plus 20 hours of prep) and I became embarrassingly lazy about learning German. It was too easy to rely on my friends for important conversations, such as with the tax office, local telecom provider, or government agencies. What I realised, though, was how I increasingly felt like I was living life in a bubble. It felt sometimes like I was invisible – when I couldn't speak to people in the bakery or supermarket, I drifted by unseen and unheard. I couldn't give thanks, couldn't complain, and couldn't ask for clarification. I was living in Germany but not living, *really* living.

Understanding the people around me, and having them understand me, opened all sorts of new doors. It enriched my experience, and enabled me to better integrate.

I know of expats who live in large cities who speak their local language (let's say, English) at work, with their friends, and at home. I once met a man who'd been in Germany six years and could not speak a single word. He'd constructed a "Little Britain," and was happy and safe inside this bubble. That's all well and good, but if you're committed to living in a new country, you've got to take that leap and learn that language.

Yes, I know – there's so much rhetoric about foreigners learning the local language (I shudder to think of incidences in Australia where people have been attacked on public transport for not speaking English,) but separate from the ultra right-wing nut-bags we regularly read about, there are practical advantages to learning the local language. Shopping is easier, for starters!

Learning a local language – and dialect – doesn't necessarily mean enrolling in a course at a local language school or CAE (council of adult education). You can learn the way I did – from watching television. Seriously! Ralf, my husband, and I used to curl up on the sofa on a Sunday afternoon and watch blockbuster films on telly, and my brain would go into sponge mode. I already knew the plots, so the words, rhythms, patterns and sounds of German washed over me. I found myself making meaning, connections. It was tiring and sometimes confusing, but never underestimate the power of your subconscious to squirrel away at language learning while your conscious mind attacks the task differently.

Another method to learn a local language also comes with the added benefit of making friends (and possibly some cash). There are Café Conversation Groups popping up all over the place, in big cities and small towns. The concept is you sit in a café, meet people wanting to learn your language (and you, of course, want to learn theirs!) and through conversation over coffee or a fine cup of tea you talk and learn. A quick look on MeetUp (search for: café conversation) will set you in the right direction, or there might be information at a local university or college.

Let's now hear from Brie and Max on the matter:

Expat Tales: Brie –American Who Lives in Germany

"I was fortunate in that I picked up German very quickly. It's still not perfect, particularly my written German and grammar, but learning the local

language even for a shorter stay abroad is essential. It helps you understand your own language better and gives you invaluable insights into the culture you've entered. A language and culture course in the actual country where you'll be working is my recommended first step. It will make acclimating far easier."

Expat Tales: Max –Kenyan who lives in Australia

"Language is definitely a factor. When you go for an interview and the language spoken is not your mother tongue, everything you say is being processed in your head before you verbally respond to a question. Obviously your thinking time and the analysis of your response will impact the actual conversation.

My advice is that you must be very open about the fact that you are speaking a foreign language and the processing time involved. Invite the interviewer to ask for more clarification when they don't understand your intended meaning.

Do not try and just speak the way you would with someone who speaks your mother tongue. Some things just don't translate word for word.

Use examples when you can't explain something."

THE T-WORD

Jacqueline

Ugh. Taxes. Okay, so while we all might complain about this dreaded "t" word, we all know that without taxes being paid, a country falls apart. Streets. Roads. Schools. Hospitals. And as I said earlier, the one government agency you don't want to go messing with is the tax office.

Before I write further, please note that this section is heavily prefaced with this caveat: *what we write here is a guide only*, and you are responsible for finding out your tax obligations! Okay, I'll get my "Serious Cap" off now, and get back to it...

I made the mistake in my first few years of living in Germany of doing my own taxes. And can I just say, for the record, that "Tax-German" is a whole different language from "German-German"! Every German I've spoken to agrees with me on this one.

Before you start working, find out the procedure for getting a TFN (tax file number). In Australia, for example, you apply from the <u>Australian Tax Office</u>, the federal agency, and it's the one number for life. In Germany, though, you apply at your local Tax Office (Finanzamt), and your number may change if you move States or municipalities, or if your employment status changes (e.g. from employee to self-employed). The only number which does not change, however, is your ID number, and that is processed centrally. So knowing the laws of the land, as it were, with regards to tax numbers and registration is important.

One more point to make with regards to tax, and to being a foreigner working abroad – find out whether your country of origin and your new country have double tax agreements. The German Federal Ministry of Finance, for example, has comprehensive information on countries with which it has (and has not) double taxation agreements. For more general information, you'll find Wikipedia is your friend and a good starting point.

Getting hit with a hefty back-payment to the tax office isn't a great experience, so we highly recommend you take the time to do your research on this point.

Kristen

Good news, Americans in the room! You are from one of only two countries in the world that require you to file and pay taxes on money made while working abroad. U-S-A!

That's right. Only the United States and Eritrea tax citizens even when they are living abroad. In the USA, this even applies to Americans who were born there but then maybe moved as a small child to another country. This means that there are actually lots of citizens who have never even filed their American taxes simply because they didn't realize they had to.

I do have one friend who will go unnamed who just stopped filing her taxes once she began working in Italy. NO, it's not *me*. I am too much of a "goody two shoes," so stop eyeballing me IRS! Down boy! Down! Anyway, my point is that I would not recommend that you just ignore your American tax situation and hope it goes away.

I personally hire someone who specializes in the tax complexities of Americans working abroad. She helps me with all the paperwork and changing rules from year to year. For the past nine years she has also filed my Italian taxes as well. Fortunately, the USA and Italy have an agreement where US citizens are not double taxed if we earn below a certain threshold (as of 2017 that's $101,300), so I was paying taxes to Italy but only Social Security contributions to the USA. Now that I have moved to Myanmar, at the moment I pay Self Employment tax and some income tax through American University of Myanmar. Whenever I am not sure of something, I ask my tax person who advises me every step of the way so I don't accidentally step in something unsavory.

For those of you who want to do your own taxes, there are a number of excellent books and software programs available for Americans abroad to get you started. One excellent resource I recently picked up is called U.S. Taxes for Worldly Americans: The Traveling Expat's Guide to Living, Working, and

Staying Tax Compliant Abroad. If you happen to be one of the many American expats who are behind on your taxes in the US and want to catch up in the most affordable and painless way possible, this book has valuable tips and advice just for you. And if you want extra peace of mind, its author Olivier Wagner, can give you a consultation and custom tax advice for your own unique situation.

Another increasingly popular option is to just give up your American citizenship! No joke. Americans who hold a second citizenship who are tired of the yearly tax fiasco are just putting up their hands in droves and turning in their passports. It may be why the American embassies have recently raised the price of renouncing citizenship.

"Renunciation of U.S. citizenship was free until July 2010, at which time a fee of **$450** was established. An increase to **$2,350**, effective September 12, 2014, was justified as 'reflective of the true cost' of processing." (That's from good ole' Wikipedia.)

In any case, I rather like being an American, even with all the cultural baggage that comes with it. So I'll put on my Girl Scout sash and start getting those returns ready for yet another year. Seriously, stop looking at me IRS. Go see what your president is up to and stop harassing me please.

Kristen

So an American woman and a Swedish woman walk into an Italian coffee bar in Rome, Italy. The first has two young children in preschool and a fulltime work contract, the other a one-year-old baby and a consultant's contract.

"My maternity leave here in Italy was so generous. I got five months leave at 100% pay and then worked part time another six months at 100% pay. Isn't Italy wonderful? In my country you only get 6-8 weeks off, no pay, and only the begrudging guarantee that you won't be fired after you return." –The American

"My maternity leave doesn't even exist here in Italy! Because I don't have a fulltime contract I get no pay and no benefits. In my home country we get *two years* of paid support after having a baby, for both men and women!" –The Swede

Yes, this was an actual conversation I had with my University Professor friend Karin from Sweden last summer in Rome.

Beauty is in the eye of the beholder and so too is the positive or negative perception of maternity, paternity, and family leave depending on where you are working and what the situation is like back in your own country.

Americans working and having children abroad are perhaps the easiest nationality to impress simply because at this time of writing we have the least generous/ non-existent maternity/paternity/family leave in the entire developed world. Swedes on the other hand come from a land where working mothers, fathers, and their families are the most supported in the world. Giving birth outside of Sweden is almost sure to be a letdown for Swedes.

It's beyond the scope of this book to get into every country's specific laws and policies for aiding parents serving in the workforce. However, it does again pay to speak to your Human Resources person at work or a local friend in your host country to learn exactly what you and your partner are entitled to where you are planted. Knowledge is power and it can give you peace of mind to know all your options.

Jacqueline

There are many benefits to being self-employed, but one glaring disadvantage is not having paid maternity leave.

By the time my son was born, I hadn't worked in some months. It had been a risky time, but despite the bumps and extended hospital trip that peppered the nine-month journey, both he and I came out healthy and strong.

However, my bank balance was telling a different story so when our son was three weeks old I had my first business meeting, at four weeks I'd started teaching, and by the time he was seven weeks old I was teaching almost full time.

It is not a path that I recommend. However, it was the only one available to us at the time.

So how can you, if you're freelancing or are self-employed, avoid this emotionally and physically difficult path? Look at your insurance (health insurance) policy and check whether you pay into a scheme that gives you a percentage of your income for a fixed period of time. Check whether there are private insurers who offer short-term funds, so you can squirrel away some cash to support you during your maternal or parental leave.

The one time in your life when you really need as little external pressure as possible is after the birth or adoption of your child, so even if the possibility of the "pitter patter of tiny feet" is far off, it pays to explore your options.

RETIREMENT AND OTHER BENEFITS

Jacqueline

In Australia, we have a <u>superannuation scheme</u> that every employed and self-employed person pays into and which builds – or should build up – into a tidy little nest egg to support us in our retirement. Now, at the time of writing this is a hot topic in Australia, as are benefits for pensioners, but let's not get political (I shall leave my growls and snarls for later!) My point is that there is a comprehensive system in place for all workers.

Here in Germany, there is also a system in place whereby a percentage of your income is put into a communal pool which can be accessed upon retirement, however I've set up a "superannuation-inspired" private scheme with Allianz (no plug intended) to complement the public scheme.

I know we're young and retirement is so far off, and I know we're footloose and fancy free, smug global trotters spinning round the world... but we're also sensible, right? And it never hurts to put some of our hard-earned cash aside for a rainy day.

Take some time to think about how a savings scheme could work for you – in your new global hotspot, do you pay into a retirement scheme with your taxes? And if you leave for your home country, will you see any benefit from those payments? Is it worth your while to set up a type of investment account into which you regularly save? What interest rates will you get? Will you have to pay tax on those savings? And can you pay into your home country's superannuation (or other) scheme while working from abroad?

Prepare a checklist of questions to ask your financial adviser, bank, or other knowledgeable person in your life and make sure you've got this squared off before you go.

CULTURE SHOCK AND SACRIFICES

Jacqueline

It's funny, but when I was a child growing up around the world, I don't remember feeling culture shock. Perhaps my world view was still forming, my perception of "normality" fluid, but whether we were surrounded by turbaned men in a bustling Chandigarh street, or eating "coconut kina" biscuits in a Papua New Guinean Highland village while the sun set, for me it was, quite simply, life.

As an adult, culture shocks come in large and small doses. The unsmiling faces on a St. Petersburg metro, the unwavering gaze of old men from eastern German apartment buildings, public consumption of alcohol on London buses and in German parks, the naked body on full display in corners of public Berlin parks... they're inconsequential, and yet they've stuck in my mind.

It's important to note, though, that culture shocks aren't necessarily negative. The capacity for, and dedication to, recycling here in Germany is breathtaking. Such efficiency, even in Berlin (where I was amazed to see <u>community composting</u> in action), was worlds away from what we had , and still have, in Australia where we are embarrassingly behind when it comes to environmental initiatives. So we have "positive shock", if we can call it that.

But focusing on the workplace, I'm reminded of the 2008 global economic crisis, and how it was managed in Germany. When the crisis hit – and it hit this region very hard – there was nervousness and fear about how the effects would be felt. Would companies fire staff? Would they cut back on training programs (including language training – my bread and butter)? How would the effects be felt in the automotive industry, which drives this region?

The answer was surprising – companies went on to reduced working hours, or *Kurzarbeit*, retaining all employees who would work just 3 or 4 days per week. And the investment in training programs, such as language training, actually *increased*. Government initiatives made this possible, and we found smaller and medium-sized enterprises in particular took advantage of the opportunity. Because increasing the capability of your workforce to better communicate in an increasingly global world meant, in the ensuing years, a stronger, more adaptable workforce who rely on more than just local customers, suppliers and partners.

How this crisis was managed in other geopolitical regions varied, but I continue to be impressed that job losses were not the first response to the downturn.

How we manage culture shock – whether we see adventure and positivity in difference, or whether we freeze and focus on negativity – is a personal thing, and sometimes we can't predict how we'll react.

Kristen, what are your thoughts here, particularly as someone who has so recently moved countries, continents, and climates?

Kristen

Well, I think that the same cultural differences, workplace culture shocks, and rude awakenings we spoke about in Chapter 2 when working in a short-term job also apply to long-term work opportunities.

You will still most likely notice that cultural norms are not like what you experienced in your home country. You may be more attuned to subtle or not so subtle discrimination at play in the workplace based on gender, race, religion, sexual orientation, or even which region of the country someone comes from.

One example from my Roman days would be that companies in Italy during the recent economic downturn fired lots of female employees because "women should be at home anyway." This was actually one of the official explanations. Say what now? That to me is culture shock.

Before moving to Myanmar last summer when I was casually browsing employment ads online, I was taken aback that the listings were specifically asking for males or females (sometimes between very specific ages) to apply. That of course is a big no-no in the United States.

And as I continue to learn about the national university system in Myanmar, I am trying to wrap my mind around professors who earn roughly only $175 USD a month, ($225 if they are senior faculty) who have no academic freedom, are not encouraged to do research, and must teach from a government-approved syllabus that cannot be changed in any way. So what that means for me is that since my field (Digital Media) has never been taught in Myanmar's universities, those government syllabi don't exist so therefore I cannot teach in the local universities in the current system.

One reason I am happy to pour my heart and soul into helping American University of Myanmar get off the ground is it is currently the only private non-profit university in the entire country. AUM is also non-religious and non-sectarian and discriminates against no one. Most Myanmar universities don't allow students with disabilities to attend (there are no accommodations made for them) and I've seen on various websites calls for applicants "no older than 20 years old." AUM must operate according to American equal opportunity standards, so it will ideally be a haven for students who don't have many doors open to them currently.

So getting back to our conversation in Chapter 2 about "rolling with the punches," you have to be aware that yes, you are not in Kansas anymore. It doesn't mean you have to take abuse or discrimination lying down, but you do have to be culturally sensitive, remember that not every country progresses at the same rate (and maybe doesn't think change is needed anyway), and you are still the odd person out as a guest in your host land.

So choosing to work in a country and culture so different from where you came from brings sacrifices. Can you live with those sacrifices is the question? Can I live with taking a pay cut to teach in Italy vs. in the USA? (Yes, but not *too much* of a pay cut.) Would I teach for the local professor's salary in Myanmar? (Sorry but no! I have international expenses not local expenses. I would volunteer to teach the occasional workshop or masterclass though.)

I tend to delight in the cultural differences that are positive. (Wow! 50 monks in training are parading down my street! Or… look at all the golden pagodas and the colorful longi skirts the women wear, etc.)

I also tend to shrug off the differences I see as negative or at least don't let them eat away at me too much. I mean I can't control the fact that there are wars or natural disasters, so why should I pull my hair out over cultural norms in my host country that I find offensive?

Every place the world over has its pros and cons. My advice is to learn as much as you can about your new home, learn what is in your control and what is not, and aim to manage your own perceptions. In other words, keep a stiff upper lip and when in doubt, stay positive and "be the change you wish to see in the world." If you are too ahead of your time for your current place of employment to deal with, consider it a lesson learned, and start thinking about moving on.

Expat Tales: Heather LaBonte Efthymiou - American Living in Cyprus, Formerly in the UK

"After I had my son we moved to Cyprus and I was going to be a 'stay-at-home' mom.

Cyprus was a huge culture shock. I am a huge animal lover and animals here, in many cases, are treated horribly. There is a lot of neglect and abuse that happens here in regards to animal welfare.

I quickly fell into animal rescue work. It was heartbreaking, inspiring, stressful, and non-stop. Yes, in the UK and USA, there is animal neglect and abuse. However, you can call the relevant authorities and, most times, something will be done about it. This is not case in Cyprus. You call the Government Vet Services in abuse cases and, most of the time, nothing is done.

Cyprus was not a good place for a California girl who loves animals to move to. The animal situation here is soul sucking. While I am proud of the work I have done, here in Cyprus, it has taken its toll on me mentally, physically, and emotionally."

Moving On

Kristen's Pre-Resignation Letter After a Decade Working in Rome

Leaving a job, especially one you've invested time, blood, sweat, and tears into for the better part of a decade is never easy… even when you know it's time to turn the page.

My university back in Rome was as supportive as any workplace could have been the day I announced that I was taking an unpaid two-year leave of absence. I explained that it was all because our time in Rome as a United Nations World Food Programme family was up and it was time to move to a duty station so my husband could get some field experience after being stranded at WFP's Roman headquarters for nine years.

Since my husband had followed me to Rome in 2006 for my shiny new job at the university, we agreed that this time it was his turn to take the lead and I would step into the role of the so-called "trailing spouse." (If you decide to get into a longer-term international career together with your partner, you too will need to become familiar with this role, who will play it, and for how long.)

As far as I knew, our time away from Rome could be as short as one year or as long as forever. Hanging onto my Roman job seemed to all concerned the only sensible thing to do despite the uncertainty. And I was grateful to even have the option and luxury of being able to change my mind.

A few months after moving to Yangon, Myanmar and over a year after having officially left the university I started getting emails about what my intentions were. Understandably they wanted to plan the upcoming academic year and were wondering out loud if they should save my full time job thousands of miles away for me or if it was time to start a new faculty search.

Full of mixed emotions, I begrudgingly sent the following reply:

"Ciao Lisa,

Thanks for your message.

I 100% understand and was wondering myself what was cooking in terms of the planning for next academic year.

Leaving a lifetime tenured contract in one of the world's most coveted cities at such a great institution with so much potential is no small matter. So, I beg your pardon if I took a long time making a final decision. It was never my intention to keep AUR in suspense.

Meanwhile my children and husband are loving Myanmar and far from hating it, I like it here as well (warts and all).

So I do believe it's time to turn the page and properly start this new chapter.

I will send a formal resignation letter within a week's time to HR. I regret I am not there in person to speak with you properly. I was planning on sneaking away to Rome from Berlin in April for a day or two so I may come by in a few months anyway.

Thanks Lisa and Richard for being such great colleagues and mentors. Please do let me know if I can ever be of assistance from *Far Far Away*. And promise we will not become strangers.

Warmest wishes and my biggest thanks,

Kristen"

And then I hit "send." Sigh.

I came down with a nasty head cold almost immediately after shutting down my computer. What did it all mean?

Kristen's Lament of the Trailing Spouse

On one hand I felt release and relief. "Today is the first day of the rest of my life," I thought.

Then again I tortured myself with, "What kind of moron gives up a lifetime tenured professor position in Rome, Italy? Hello? Anyone home?"

And yet, it may not have made logical sense, but it *felt* right. Thank you intuition.

I of course can only follow my own heart. I can't tell you what is best for *you*. But despite my own choices I think it's best to warn again upfront, living and working abroad is no easy task. You will make sacrifices. But also keep in mind that *not* travelling or working abroad is another type of sacrifice in the name of maintaining a sense of "security."

The reason I even had a lifetime contract in Rome with all the fancy titles is because even though my husband and I got itchy feet again after just four years in Italy, We. Could. Not. Move. No. Matter. How. Hard. We. Tried.

We used to joke that there are far worse places to be stuck than in Rome, Italy and yet there we were for another six years. Those were the years when we started our family and got spooked at how difficult it was to have two full time jobs and small babies in a foreign land with no grandparents around to help.

But those extra six years of stagnation turned out to be a gift. One curse of having the travel bug is you often don't stay in any one place long enough to advance in your career properly or put down roots. I received tenure and two promotions as well as a whole host of managerial responsibilities at my university simply because I was there (and was good!) for an extended period of time. Fate had me bloom where I was planted and so I did my best.

So with the exception of those jobs where you *are* expected to move every few years (International Schools, the United Nations, certain non-profit organizations like *Save the Children*, etc.) finally up and leaving your long-term job can leave you feeling a tad lost.

I understand. I've been there. I am there. But thankfully, "fortune befriends the bold" and I am fine. I think I may even be better than fine. And that's my hope for you as well should you decide to move on from your long-term job abroad. Just remember that everything you've done to date makes you that much more qualified and ready for your next challenge.

Onward ho!

Kristen

If you decide to work your way around the world with your partner or significant other, you may find that one of you ends up with a larger salary, better perks, or with "an opportunity you *both* can't refuse."

My husband followed me to Rome when I started at The American University of Rome, and now I in turn have followed him to Myanmar. But will I be the next one to take the lead after his four-year contract ends? Possibly. But it's starting to get complicated, especially with children now in the mix.

For one, the UN's *World Food Programme* currently provides 85% school tuition support for employees' children from ages 5 through the university years. Yes, that even applies to those horribly expensive American universities. (The UN keeps adjusting their benefits so we can't be sure they will be still be this generous when our own kids are ready for university.)

In any case, even the prospect that our children might be able to attend university at a fraction of the cost is enough to make us think twice about Michael leaving the UN system any time soon. (They could also just go to school in Germany practically for free. Problem solved!)

But one thing less positive we have noticed amongst friends and colleagues working for the UN is there are an awful lot of broken marriages, high divorce rates, and estranged children scattered about the globe.

Yes, this following your spouse from country to country every few years can take an emotional toll. The UN actually calls employee's spouses "dependents" even if we are employed full time. This is insulting enough for anyone, but my entrepreneur friend Daniel (a Canadian) in Myanmar has followed his UN aid-worker wife to four countries now and still resents this term as violently as I do. How *dare* they call us that! Even worse, if we want to visit our loved ones at their office we must wear a badge with our name, photo, and the word "dependent" written in large bold text below.

In any case, the temporary nature of this type of UN work often calls for a move every few years that then disrupts the "trailing spouse's" still new work situation while the UN employee continues to advance and climb the career ladder. Children must be yanked out of school and transplanted anew. Depending on their ages, this can also be quite traumatic, especially during the high school years.

I bring this all up because it is what I am going through now. I don't regret my decision to come to Myanmar, but I am well aware of the tightrope we are currently walking on. I also know myself (and children) enough to know that perhaps we may have to find a more permanent posting in the years ahead for our entire family's sake!

Anyway, let's hear now from my friend Luisa, a distinguished Professor of Education with thirty years of experience teaching around the world. She is also a trailing spouse and coming to terms with yet another reinvention of herself, now in Myanmar.

Expat Tales: Dr. Luisa Illescas-Glascock -Mexican Who Used to Live in the USA and China, Now Living in Myanmar

"I became a 'trailing spouse' when my husband got a teaching position job in East Asia and we moved from the USA to former Burma.

My career came to a pause. I am an educator as well but there was no job offer for me. I had to shift my mind from seeing myself as an independent professional to becoming a dependent wife, or 'trailing spouse.'

The absence of a formal job meant assuming a role with possibilities of waking up late, preparing our meals, and being in charge of housekeeping.

In my marriage, this was the same role my husband would have assumed if it had been the other way around -moving because of my job.

The novelty of not having to work amused me and pleased me for a couple of months. I could do anything I wanted during the day hours. However, soon I felt the limitation of not having a set routine or a place of work I was expected to be at.

As much as I enjoyed the freedom of not having predictable work hours and doing things at my own pace like reading the newspaper in the middle of the day or my workout at any time. The fact is that I cannot get used to being a 'trailing spouse.'

I feel the need to have my mind engaged in some modality in my profession, to earn my own income, and to contribute to my family beyond domestic chores. It is for my own sake, emotionally and financially, that I will pursue engagement in my professional life as much as possible in my new setting."

The strains of living abroad and/or moving frequently can affect any marriage or family. Let's hear now from Heather who cautions against navigating life by just following your heart only.

Expat Tales: Heather LaBonte Efthymiou - American Living in Cyprus, Formerly in the UK

"Here in Cyprus, there is not much work as it is a small island with less than a million people. Cyprus has way more educated people than jobs.

I cannot work in cigarette smoke, which severely limits me for work here. I never had any concern about this as I had planned to be a stay-at-home mom.

I ended up getting a divorce and now it is a big concern. I am, ultimately, looking for online work that I can do from home. This will give me some flexibility and will keep me away from cigarette smoke (it is everywhere here in Cyprus). I am regretting not getting a University degree after high school, as it would have given me more opportunities to work online.

I actually regret moving to Europe. I moved here for love and did not ever think I would end up divorced. When you move to another country and have children; if it does not work out, you cannot move back to your country and take the children with you. Many people do not think about this until it's too late. I am 'trapped' on this island for another 15 years until my son finishes school. It is a sentence I cannot completely wrap my head around. So please take extreme caution when getting into a relationship in the foreign country you move to as love doesn't always conquer all. There are serious consequences involved."

TYING UP LOOSE ENDS WITHOUT LOSING YOUR MIND

Kristen

Always consult with your Human Resources Office at your job as your first resource when dealing with the complexities of closing shop. However, a few main questions you will need to consider when leaving your job are:

- **When is your official "last day?"**
  In Italy I learned, the process was not as easy as sending a resignation letter like in the US. There was an 8-step online process and Italian bureaucracy to go through (of course!) Every country and workplace is different so don't just quit and assume everything takes care of itself.

- **What happens to your retirement account?**
  If you are leaving your host country, how can you still claim your money? If you are staying in your host country, what steps do you need to take if any?

- **What taxes do you still need to file?**
  What are your tax obligations in your host country as well as at home? Even if you are leaving your host country, you may still have tax liabilities. Knowledge is power so find out!

These are of course the three biggest questions. Smaller ones include courtesies like who will take over your work responsibilities, how will your employer transition away from your services, will you close up your bank, etc.

I'm in the process of making an online course and book on the very process of making this major transition as smooth and easy as possible. In the meantime, we have some free videos on our <u>Free At Last YouTube Channel</u> that show my recent transition from Rome to Myanmar and all the steps in between. You are most welcome to join us there, laugh at my misadventures, and ask us your own specific questions!

SOME FINAL KEY POINTS TO REMEMBER

- **Flexibility is key.**
  Whether you have lined up your new job already from your home country, are being transferred, or plan to find work once you arrive in your new country, expect the unexpected. The work culture, the job market, your new coworkers, and even the workplace rules may be wildly different than what you are used to. Having a positive can-do attitude and a sense of humor will always be an asset. It is likely that your new work situation will not match the daydream you had in your head, and more often than not, that turns out to be just fine.

- **Make sure you are prepared for the local job market and workplace culture by doing**

your homework. Find out what the local differences are when it comes to what should and should not be on your CV and what qualifications are expected for particular jobs. Learn what the rules and "secret handshakes" are for your new company or organization. Find a mentor in your new host country or speak with other expats in person or online in Facebook groups or in *InterNations*. Networking can also be a great way to gain valuable information and insights.

- **If you are moving together with a partner or with children, be prepared for more complexity.** If you have itchy feet and the desire to move ASAP, be sensitive to the needs of your partner or children who may not be as ready as you are to uproot. Respect the opinions, needs, and concerns of all members of your family and weigh those together when making any kind of life-altering decisions. You may find that certain family members get priority depending on what is happening in their lives at the time. For example, a husband may choose to let their wife take the lead if he is ready for a change and she has supported his career for many years (or vice-versa) or both parents may try and stay put in a country until both kids graduate from high school before moving on again, etc.

- **Don't forget to tidy up!** Leaving a job is never as simple as it seems. Make sure you understand what you need to do to successfully make an exit without everything falling apart back at the office. Get information about your final paychecks, bank account, retirement plan, what taxes you may owe, etc. before jumping on that next airplane into the wide blue yonder.

A long-term job or career abroad is a fantastic way to gain new skills while exploring a new country like a local. But what if those doors you've been knocking on just don't want to open? What if the idea of starting your own business abroad is really more your cup of tea? Let's explore the possibilities in the next chapter.

CHAPTER 5: STARTING A BUSINESS ABROAD

"If opportunity doesn't knock, build a door."
–Milton Berle

GETTING STARTED AND SETTING UP

Jacqueline

There are many different reasons for considering starting your own business abroad. It could be that a fierce independent streak steers you away from working for "the man," your preferred business model is non-existent where you're located, you're nervous about inflicting your fledgling foreign language skills on an employer, or there are no work opportunities for your skill set so you make your own.

And starting a new business can simply be something you stumble into in order to survive. That's how it happened to me.

After stumbling into language training, getting qualified, and realising I loved it (and the country I'd just bought a house in,) I popped in to teach one day only to find out I'd been fired.

Oh. With a mortgage and suddenly no working visa, reality kicked in after the self-pitying hangover slunk off. A quick trip to the immigration office and a change of visas (from Working Visa to Fiancée Visa) meant I didn't have to leave within 24 hours. But what on earth was I going to do?

As Ralf, my Ralf (the reason for the Fiancée Visa,) wisely said: keep teaching. We looked online at how to set myself up, what the Tax Office rules were, whether I needed to be registered with the regional Chamber of Commerce, what the insurance requirements were, and finally we nabbed a URL and started optimising a simple web site.

It is as much of a leap starting your own business abroad as it is at home, but when going through the process abroad I have a few tips:

- **Keep an open mind**, especially in regards to differing legislation, reporting requirements, insurance, and tax obligations.

- **Stay positive**. You may be thrust into opening your own business, but it can be successful with good planning, positivity, hard work, and humour.

- **Create a sales funnel** that is simple, elegant, and easy to find. This means a website with optimised text, which is easy to navigate that lets customers easily find and contact you, and which provides samples of your work or feedback from existing clients.

Jacqueline and Ralf getting married in Plauen, Germany. 2009.

One of the advantages I had was that my husband is a SEM (Search Engine Marketing) professional, having worked in SEM/SEA for a decade. Plus, he's a native German speaker. This meant he could not only build and write my initial webpage, but also ensure the pages were search-engine friendly. After going "live," I had my first nibble within ten days, and first two signed-up clients within two weeks. Within three months I was fully booked, and within six months over-booked.

Going solo, launching your own business, means you're solely responsible for tax payments and insurance, including (though you would have to check this in your specific location) retirement contributions and VAT (depending on your level of income.) My top tip, (and don't underestimate this please) is to find a good, reliable accountant. Your business can only benefit from a healthy, positive relationship with the Tax Office and though an accountant costs money, it can absolutely save you money. Trust me, I speak from first-hand experience!

So let's pop those tips into dot points for you:

- **Ensure your visa allows you to be self-employed.**

- **Register as self-employed with the Tax Office.**

- **Advise your health insurance provider that you're self-employed.**

- **Engage the services of a competent accountant.** (Ask about their fee schedule before signing on the dotted line, and whether they act as a go-between for you and the Tax Office.)

- **Map out your business plan**: what goods or services will you offer, where are your clients (who is your tribe?), how will they find you, and how will you find them?

- **Design, write, and optimise an elegant website**. (If you need help with a site in the local language, site design or SEO text, there are multiple quality providers on Fiverr who won't break the bank.)

- **Utilise contacts you already have**, so if – like me – you were working for one company and are now going solo, send your clients a courtesy email to let them know how they can stay in touch with you. Be careful though, not to breach any non-competition clauses in any contract you may have had with your former employer.

It's not an exhaustive list, but it certainly gives you a solid starting point for spreading your wings and following that self-employed dream.

But enough from me for now, let's hear from someone else who has made it work. Sweety, over to you!

Expat Tales: Sweety -Indian Living in the USA

"After I was done with my studies I got an offer at my boyfriend's (now husband's) company. His boss had heard about me and the way I am. He just offered me an internship for one summer. I never went there for an interview or even had a phone call with him.

In that job I got exposure to real corporate life where I was able to meet so many people and learn a lot of new things. After working there for almost three years, I got employed at an engineering company as a Junior Engineer. I was going to a lot of networking groups through the company and made some great contacts and built great relationships with the clients. And then I got promoted to Director of Public Relations and Marketing.

Working directly with the clients gave me an idea that I can do something on my own and after giving it some thought, I started my own business."

FINDING AND KEEPING CLIENTS

Jacqueline

Finding your first client can be daunting, but it needn't be. Remember when we spoke about networking earlier? Here is where your networking skills come into play.

That said, it does all depend on what it is you're doing. When I first started as a solo businesswoman, although I'd already been working and teaching in Germany for three years, I hadn't collected (nor been permitted to) collect contact details from my clients. Further, as I was in a new geographical area I needed to start from scratch.

What helped attract my first client was a simple, targeted and keyword-optimised website my then fiancé designed for me. Until then, there were no native English-speaking, experienced, and qualified language trainers in the area, so we did our research, uploaded the page, and within a week I had my first call.

However, as we know, a phone call or even a meeting aren't signatures on the dotted line. And this is where your personality comes into play, and understanding the core needs of your future clients. What do they really need which they can't put into words? I'm not talking about their pain points, but what intangible *"je ne sais quoi"* are they looking for?

From my side of things, it's sunshine. Plain and simple, my clients aren't just looking to improve their English communication skills, but they're looking for sunshine in their training sessions. It helps that I genuinely like all my clients and that I genuinely care about them. The sunshine comes naturally. And that's been my secret to success, and why the same clients who signed up all those years ago are still clients today.

So, my top tips here? Find a way for your future clients to find you – is it a website? Blog? Fiverr profile? Make it good (content is king), make it optimized (see previous comment about content), and make it unarguably *you*.

Know yourself, know your tribe, be yourself, and success will follow.

Kristen

Like Jacqueline, in my experience it also pays to research and understand the unique and specific needs of your host country. So for example, now that I am doing live workshops, master classes, and events here in Yangon, Myanmar, I have to reach prospective clients the Myanmar way.

In a country where only 3.5% of people have access to a computer, it means that having a great website would not help me here with the locals since most people rarely visit an actual website. In this country where the Internet was available to the masses for the first time only since 2014, it's all about Facebook being accessed from a Smartphone. So when I need to get the word out and I am trying to reach a target audience of Myanmar prospective students (or Myanmar employers looking to train their staff), I use my Facebook page (with or without Facebook ads) in place of a website.

Conversely, if I want to reach the expat crowd (another target audience), I use my website, Facebook page, Twitter feed, and some strategic postings in Yangon expat groups (on Facebook, Google+, and LinkedIn).

So, as Jacqui mentioned earlier, once you have your business plan and paperwork in order, you should sit down and really think about *who* you are trying to reach.

Please don't say "everyone." That's not a good enough answer. Think nationality (are they a local in your host country or in the expat community for example). Think ages, genders, occupations, income levels, and interests.

At the moment I am planning an upcoming "Early Career Development Workshop" that will help Myanmar students, recent graduates, and junior employees learn how to look for and apply for jobs, how to set up their CVs, and how to present themselves to prospective employers. I know (with the help of a local Myanmar female business leader) that this target audience has never had any kind of career training in school, they come from limited financial means, and they will most likely need Burmese/English translations during the presentation. Being clear about who my target audience is helps me not only plan the best services for them but also informs how I will reach and recruit them.

So don't forget to think about this for your business as well and know that you can also have more than one target audience at any given time depending on what you are selling or offering.

Jacqueline

In business, as in life, a little diplomacy can go a long way. We adapt our norms to those around us. A former client of mine, Elvira, is an absolute powerhouse of a woman. She's tall, has a mane of blazing red hair, flashing green eyes, and she's built herself up from nothing to owning a chain of successful physiotherapy practices here in Germany. She's intelligent, tough, independent, and witty. I have such a soft spot for her.

Now, a few years ago Elvira had the idea of expanding her physiotherapy practice into the United Arab Emirates. She wanted to link with hotels, and have her company's services available to guests (in addition to traditional massage, she thought therapeutic treatments would be of value).

So Elvira went to the UAE, sourced a male business partner, learned some Arabic, learned some finer cultural points, and over the course of the next 18 months closed some important deals. She embodied what Kristen and I have talked about in this book – do your research, embrace difference as a positive, and be diplomatic. Homework is rewarded.

Whether cultural differences be gender-based, age-based, race- or religion-based, or other, you'll need to find out how far you personally can bend and weave, and where your diplomatic breaking point is.

Before we move on, let's hear from our author, instructor, and entrepreneur friend Barrett who details how she dealt with her own diplomatic breaking point in a positive way when living in Denmark.

Expat Tales: Barrett Clemmensen Powell - American who recently returned to the USA after living in Denmark

"The expat life brings lots of new and unexpected things into your life. It also brings things you subconsciously hope not to see, hear, or experience.

I moved to Copenhagen, Denmark in pursuit of another academic degree (I already had a masters in theology and pastoral clinical care and two other undergraduate degrees.) Denmark appealed to me because I could deepen my psychology and cultural background experience with academia. I got quite the education in both, Danish-style!

I met so many Danes who love to meet people from other cultures and explore the world. I embraced the language and the customs.

Living in a country that has several times been named the land of the world's happiest people, I was nonetheless surprised to come across ethnic discrimination that I never thought I would see in Denmark.

I remember the cold winter days standing at the bus stop facing huge ads, some taller than me, which spewed hate. They generated anxiety and fear against Poles and others from former Eastern European countries. So often I heard from politicians, read in newspapers, and heard on the street comments about how Poles are inferior to Danes, uneducated compared to Danes, and worst of all, were stealing jobs from Danes.

Poles and those from former Eastern Europe were portrayed in Denmark like Mexicans often are in the USA. I was shocked and saddened. During those same cold Danish winter days while studying at university there, it was the Polish exchange students who always took time to talk to me, share some 'hygge' (the Danish word for coziness) with me via an unscheduled cup of coffee or invitation to gather. We would talk about our academic classes and projects and share laughs at warm and cozy apartment party evenings.

One sunny icy midwinter day, as they were preparing to return to their native land, they invited me to visit them in Poland. A few years later I did call those same former classmates and I was welcomed into their homes and lives in Poland with warmth and love. I found it to be both a beautiful country and an even more beautiful group of people. I love people. I love our differences, idiosyncrasies, and uniqueness.

My solution to the problem of this ethnic hatred was to reach deep into my heart and with other expatriates start creating intercultural gatherings that brought together the many Danes with the internationals living and working in Copenhagen.

The high point, one of my joys, has been to conceive and oversee a Polish festival in Copenhagen that showcases the brilliance and talent that Poland is producing in the world in the fields of literature, intellectual debate, music (particularly jazz) etc.

Danes are embracing it. In the midst of nation-state hatred and a world that seems to be increasingly succumbing to hate and polarization, there are Danes, Poles, and others coming out for a celebration of Polish culture and the ties between Denmark and Poland. It took an American living and working abroad to help make it happen and I think of it as one of my contributions to humanity as a global citizen."

Thanks Barrett! Now let's turn our attention back to business and think about how we might expand our operation.

EXPANDING AND SCALING UP

Jacqueline

So you've got your first clients, you've woven your way through cultural differences, and you've got your diplomat's cap firmly on your head. Fabulous. But now you've reached capacity, possibly gone over, and you're ready to take the next steps with your business.

First thing to consider: *how* can you expand? If you're offering a service, expansion naturally means bringing more people on board. Is there actually the demand for that, and how would your role change? If you do bring someone or some people on board, what labour laws (if any) do you need to adhere to, and are you permitted to do this in the first place? As always, do your homework.

Second thing to consider, and this refers to a question from above: what will your new role be? If you're expanding and bringing new people on board, will you continue the direct client contact you've had to date, or move into planning / management? Are you prepared for that, and will your clients accept a new face?

I'm at this stage at the moment, actually, as my teaching business has expanded to the point where I can't manage it all alone. I've got new teachers on board and am considering transitioning the last of my direct clients to a new teacher. It makes economic sense, however as I said earlier, I genuinely like my students.

So there is an emotional aspect of this expansion decision to consider too. I will honestly miss seeing my students once I hand over all teaching. I'll miss their stories, their enthusiasm, their humour, and the rapport each group has. However, it really is time. Yes, I am sighing as I write this.

But, I digress. This section is about *you* and not me, the decisions you have to make and the homework you have to undertake before making those decisions.

- What will expansion mean?

- Is there enough business to justify bringing people on board?

- How will the structure of your business change?

- Will your clients accept the change? How can you reassure them it will be "business as usual"?

- What formal processes (e.g. with your tax office, employment office, insurance provider or chamber of commerce) do you need to undertake?

- Are you prepared to hand over tasks and responsibility and to be a leader?

- Are you emotionally ready for the change?

SOME FINAL KEY POINTS TO REMEMBER

- **Get all your permissions and make a plan, Stan.** Find out if your particular visa allows you to become self-employed in your host country. If so, inform the tax man or woman, your medical insurance company, set up your business plan (complete with mission and vision statements), and get started looking for a competent accountant to help you with your books. One easy invoice service for small businesses you might try is called Aynax. Free trials are available online.

- **Know your target audience/ideal customer well.** Ask yourself how old they are, what is their occupation, income or education level, and gender, etc.? Think about what their interests might be. What are their biggest hopes and dreams? What is holding them back and how might you be the potential answer to their unique problems?

- **Create an easy way for your ideal customers to find and contact you.** This could be some or all of the following: a Facebook page, a well-crafted website, a LinkedIn Profile, advertising in social media groups where your ideal customers hang out, etc. Great offline essentials include: professional-looking business cards, flyers, and good old-fashioned word of mouth referrals.

- **As your business begins to take off, change may be afoot.** If you find yourself with more and more clients or gigs than your sanity can handle, it might be time to hire employees whom you will outsource tasks to. If this is the case, speak with your tax person and accountant to find out what paperwork needs to be done to best accommodate these changes legally and ethically.

OK. We've dived into the world of starting a business abroad, but what if you want to create a portable business that is just as mobile as you are?

You may just be a budding full or part-time digital nomad. Pack your laptop, bring an extra power cable, pick up another SIM card, and read on!

Chapter 6: Taking Your Location-Independent Business With You Wherever You Go as a Digital Nomad

"I may not have gone where I intended to go, but I think I have ended up where I intended to be." — Douglas Adams

What Exactly is a Digital Nomad and Would You Actually Want to Be One?

Kristen

When I picture a nomad in my mind's eye, I think of a camel caravan traipsing across the Sahara Desert in search of the next campsite before sundown. So when I think of a *digital nomad,* I see a lone figure holding a laptop while riding that camel. She/he is probably looking for a Wi-Fi hotspot and a power source.

Wikipedia states: "**Digital nomads** are individuals who use telecommunications technologies to earn a living and, more generally, conduct their life in a **nomadic** manner." (*The big, traditional dictionaries like *Oxford's* and *Merriam-Webster's* only have "digital" and "nomad" listed as separate words. Maybe this will be the year they add the term to show they are with the times?)

So, while I hate to put labels on myself, it seems that I may in fact be a digital nomad or at least a part-time digital nomad wannabe, given that I do freelance art and design for clients, consulting work for online and traditional educational institutions, write eBooks, and sell online courses to people all over the world regardless of where I am living. The only thing getting in the way of course is Myanmar's impossibly slow Internet connection.

Jacqueline

Our internet is somewhat faster than Myanmar's, and I've also got online courses and eBooks, but in my mind, I'm a common-or-garden expat, squirreling out a life in the old East Germany. Digital Nomads are too cool for this school!

Though…. gosh it would be great to be one. However, I've got roots which stretch too deep – a house, a business, and a fabulous school for my son. As much as I love travel, I have to admit the nomadic life is no longer for me. And there's nothing wrong with having the creature comforts, or desiring them. Neighbours with whom you can while away the long summer evenings in the garden, the chimney-sweep who has a new story every year, the lady at the bakery who knows exactly which rye bread rolls you like, and the long-term clients who always know to expect a hand-made Christmas card in December. But despite my being able to work in any corner of the globe, I've found my happy place. (Until the next hard winter, that is! Then it's off to the sunshine!)

Jacqueline with students and a silly hat. -Germany, 2013.

This concept of the nomadic lifestyle naturally brings us to looking more closely at how we can earn money to support ourselves when home is anywhere we lay our hat.

First, though, some advice from Andrea on being location independent:

Expat Advice: Andrea, Lead Data Strategist - American working in the USA and sub-Saharan Africa

> *"Learn how to work with your team in a lean online way. Using What's App groups, Asana for task tracking, Dropbox, weekly Google hangout meetings, and other tools that are really helpful for sharing things make it easy for your team to work*

from anywhere in the world and still communicate."

HOW TO MAKE A LIVING WHEN YOU DON'T LIVE ANYWHERE? THE MANY OPTIONS

Kristen

So let's now explore the many part time, slap-dash, and full time possibilities for being a digital nomad.

This is a non-exhaustive list of possibilities for what you might do as a digital nomad. Choose the option(s) that most gel with your own area of expertise, skill set, education level, and overall enthusiasm and see where it takes you.

- Create online courses (Try udemy.com, skillshare.com, ofcourse.com, curious.com, Thinkific, Zenler, teachable, and others.)

- Write blog articles for companies

- Do freelance art or design

- Become a digital assistant (e.g. through Fiverr.com)

- Do social media marketing for companies and entrepreneurs

- Fix, create, or optimize websites

- Create an SEO (Search Engine Optimization) keyword business

- Write e-books and record audio books.

- Participate in paid research studies

- Be a freelance copyeditor

- Become a ghost writer

- Do translations

- Be an academic tutor

- Create a free online store that sells your designs as t-shirts, art prints, tech accessories, and more. (Try society6.com, threadless.com, cafepress.com and others to start.)

- Check out the more unusual gigs and services on Fiverr.com (and sites like Fiverr) to become inspired to start your own

- Create classroom and teacher products and must-haves over at teacherspayteachers.com

- Become an online affiliate with advertising on your own blog or website

The list could go on and on. It's beyond the scope of this book to get into the specific "hows and whys" of each possibility, so if you see an option that piques your interest, I encourage you to learn more about getting started through books, courses, and joining online communities of people already successfully doing it.

You might also get inspiration by having a look at some *Design Thinking* free PDF worksheets available online from IDEO and Stanford Design School.

Design Thinking is a system for becoming more innovative, flexible, and creative. To go over it in a nutshell:

- **First you check in with a problem you might be having.** (Ex. I need a location independent job!)

- **Next you begin brainstorming and jotting down possibility after possibility.** Here it's all about the quantity of ideas. Just come up with as *many* ideas as possible. Don't fuss over any of them yet and don't censor yourself.

- **Then, you look at your list and start to choose something that resonates with you.** Begin to hone in on one or two possibilities you might try. This is going to be your prototype. (Ex. Set up a website and start offering copyediting services there and on Fiverr to start.)

- **It's time for action!** This is your testing phase. Design Thinkers learn by doing instead of theorizing and sitting around asking "what if?"

Many of us have been trained at an early age to fear failure. With Design Thinking failure is a good thing! Here we take one of our ideas and we just DO IT! Will we make mistakes? Absolutely. It's all good.

Try out your idea. See what works and what doesn't. See what you like and what you dislike. Then fine-tune your prototype based on both the positive and negative feedback you got.

- **Rinse and repeat.** Keep at it. Did you know that it took Thomas A. Edison 10,000 tries to invent the light bulb? He never saw himself as failing. He famously said, "I have not failed. I've just found 10,000 ways that won't work." That's the spirit of a Design Thinker!

"Fail often so you can succeed sooner." —Tom Kelley, Ideo partner

Keep at it and use every experience as a lesson for moving forward.

THE IMPORTANCE OF INTUITION

Kristen

Here I'm going to cheat a little bit and share with you some advice and inspiration from my friend Amber

Shannon who is actually living and working in her home country, the USA.

Amber is a *Professional Intuitive and Conscious Lifestyle Guide* and can be found online at www.Amberlina.com. She has many happy clients from all over the world and could run her business from anywhere.

Domestic Digital Nomad Tales: Amber Shannon - *Just Moved Back to Fort Lauderdale, Florida after Living in California*

> *"I was first introduced to the idea of creating a location independent business through reading 'The 4-Hour Workweek' by Tim Ferris.*
>
> *Being someone that never fit in with the mainstream corporate culture, I knew that being able to live my passion full-time, from anywhere in the world was the right lifestyle for me. I've been doing it since 2013 and I can't imagine living any other way! It's given me the flexibility to make quick moves, including most recently when a family member needed support and care. I was able to easily make the move and be there for my family without any hesitation.*
>
> *Since my work is in the realm of personal growth and spirituality, my advice for others seeking a location independent business or lifestyle is from*

that perspective, and based on my own life experience. Here is my absolute best advice:

Hone your intuition. This should really be a top priority for everyone, no matter your business or lifestyle choice, but especially for those looking to live or work abroad. I like to define intuition as your personal connection to infinite wisdom and trustworthy guidance. It can help you with everything from choosing dinner to saving your life!

The ability to think logically and rationally is extremely valuable, but those abilities have a certain limit. If you want to follow your passion and really live the life of your dreams (safely!), you must also be able to tap into and use your instincts.

Your intuitive senses work in the same way as your physical senses, but they work for the energetic or "non-physical" world around you. For example, they can tell you whether the intentions of those around you are potentially harmful. They also work for future planning, by being able to sense whether a situation 'feels' right. These are just two examples, but they give you an idea of the incredible value the intuition can provide in the life of a digital nomad.

There are four primary intuitive senses, commonly known as "the four clairs." They are simply different channels through which intuitive or instinctive knowledge can come to you. They differ in the same way that seeing, hearing, and touching are all different channels through which you receive information about the physical components of the environment around you.

The Four Clairs are:

- *Claircognizance, which means "clear knowing"*

- *Clairvoyance, which means "clear seeing"*

- *Clairaudience, which means "clear hearing"*

- *Clairsentience, which means "clear feeling"*

We were all born with strong intuitive senses, but since our current society is predominantly focused on the physical world, we are taught to rely solely on our physical senses. For most people, this creates a fading of intuitive awareness. However, our intuition is with us for life, and we can strengthen our experience of it by having a clear desire and cultivating it through a variety of practices.

The best and most effective practice I know to strengthen intuition is meditation. There are many ways to meditate, so I encourage you to try a few different styles and see which one you like best. Whatever you do, don't force yourself to do it! Meditating should be an enjoyable experience, so if you're not enjoying it, switch to a new style.

Sending you the best of intentions as you follow your passion and experience all of the joy and magnificence this beautiful planet has to offer!"

BUT WHAT HAPPENS WHEN THE INTERNET GOES OUT?

Kristen

"You're moving where?" people asked incredulously when I told them I was moving to Yangon, Myanmar. The question would often come with an echo, "Myanmar?" usually followed by, "Wait. Where's that?"

Myanmar, a country bordering India, China, Bangladesh, Thailand, and Laos is waking up from decades of international isolation, military rule, and sanctions. It boasts a lush, unspoiled natural landscape rich with minerals and natural resources. Its people, probably its greatest resource, are by far among the friendliest I've met anywhere in the world.

It's also currently among the poorest countries in Asia (though hopefully that will one day change) and only 3.5% of the population has access to a computer. Only 6% have access to the Internet. If you *are* one of the lucky 6%, the Internet you have access to is shaky at best and completely out and unavailable at worst. The situation is much better in the larger cities and as mentioned before, more and more people in Myanmar are getting connected via their cell phones, with Facebook being their top destination of choice.

Anyway, shortly after moving to Myanmar, I was alarmed at how often the Internet was out completely and tried to come to terms with the fact that my "digital nomad" online business was going to be severely compromised.

In other words, my little growing enterprise I worked so hard to build these past two years so I could take it with me no matter where in the world I went was... um...just a tad at risk. (I can see the Asia-savvy digital nomads in my Facebook group who warned me about Myanmar's Internet access shaking their heads sadly... They told me to move to Thailand, but that's not going to happen any time soon.)

Sure, luckily I can still write blog posts offline, make an illustration, or record a video lesson without the Internet. In fact, if anything good can be said for having the Internet go out randomly several times a day, it's that it forces me to concentrate on tasks without the threat of email, Facebook, Twitter, CNN, and other distractions constantly competing for my attention. I call it "Forced Focus" and that is a positive.

Because I'm 10 to 13 hours ahead of most people I need to communicate with online (mostly in the USA), I often schedule Skype calls, webinars, and other meetings for the very early or very late hours.

My Internet had gone out at 2PM yesterday. Due to "Forced Focus" I did some video work for The American University of Myanmar and ran errands. When I came back at 6PM it was still not up and running. I've been trying to make sense of when and why it goes out so I can plan better for the future but there appears to be no rhyme or reason. I'm told that things like the weather, time I go on, and even the wind can be to blame. I thought I actually had things all figured out, planning in advance and testing Skype, and Zoom.us (for webinars) just to ensure I could have a shot at beaming myself into the online realm.

When I worry/plan the most though is when I'm scheduled to teach live webinars for the UN"s *University for Peace*. I time the hour-long lectures for 9AM EST (8:30PM for me in Yangon) so that none of the worldwide participants across all time zones have to try and attend between midnight and 5AM. *Zoom* has actually proven to be a reliable and forgiving (of bad connections) webinar tool and so far (knock on wood) I've been able to somehow deliver.

Plan B however is that I now always buy a little pin drive with SIM card so I can use a "plug and play" type of Internet access as backup. I did this in Ethiopia last year when I was teaching university there and it worked fairly well, at least for most basic tasks. I won't even get into how long it takes in the developing world to upload and download things. My solution is just start uploading/downloading overnight and hope to not wake up to an error message.

Anyway, that is the current situation. And really it all seems so trivial in the face of the extreme poverty that exists in Myanmar as well as the fact that access to safe water, enough food, and electricity (which goes out many times a day) is an even bigger, more pressing problem for the population. I mean really, who am I to even complain?

Ever the optimist, I will say that this experience is overall a good one. It has forced me to find other ways to work and be of service in my new country. I never wanted to be holed up in a home office anyway away from everyone and everything just outside my door. Without speedy Internet access I'm actually creating an even stronger connection to this wonderful country through in-person (imagine that!) teaching, volunteering, and collaborations.

Yes, on second thought, a little offline time never hurt anyone. Thanks for the lesson Myanmar!

Expat Tales: Justin P. Moore -American Living in Germany and author of *The Lotus and the Artichoke* series of vegan cookbooks.

> *"As with any business, so many things are about timing and receptivity as they are about motivation and determination.*
>
> *My shift from being a graphic designer and artist in the gallery scene to being a cookbook author (designing and photographing my own books*

inspired by my travels) was effective not only because I worked hard to make it happen and involved many of my passions, but because food and travel became increasingly popular (especially in social media and blogs) in the last few years.

Specializing in vegan food and making things very personal worked well for me, too, adding a strong element of uniqueness to an already popular and in demand field.

Lastly, building a community of support and reaching out to as many like-minded cookbook authors and food/travel bloggers as possible, as well as diving into Crowdfunding (to help finance independent projects and find new audiences worldwide) made things more enjoyable, exciting, and effective."

PLAN B

Kristen

Let's face it; having a traditional, location-based business as well as a virtual, location-independent business is not for the faint of heart. People try and succeed, but more often than not, try and fail all the time.

In particular, if you are used to the security that a monthly paycheck at a traditional job working for someone else brings in, then the insecurity and wild fluctuations of pay each month running your own business will take some getting used to, to say the least!

I originally started my foray into the "online sharing economy" as nothing more than a fun experiment and as a bit of research while I was still teaching at my university full time back in late 2014.

Now over two years in and no longer with the security of my university's monthly paycheck, I marvel at how far I've come as well as shake my head that good ole' sensible me has allowed myself to become this "wild and crazy."

You might remember how I quit my lifetime tenured Associate Professor job after ten years living and working in Rome, Italy. What I've essentially done is "thrown away" the dream that nearly every sane part time and full time professor aspires to: job security, benefits, pretty-sounding titles, and the old fashioned notion that one can work in the same place for decades on end until retirement or death. Seriously, what is my problem?

Well, I've never been like the other kids. Most of us afflicted with wanderlust or who have a drive to live a life less ordinary have trouble with a typical cookie-cutter future all mapped out for us. We get itchy feet for better and for worse.

As mentioned before in Chapter 4, experts say that expats and those of us who marry across cultures also have a higher chance of getting a divorce. I can absolutely see that. For it makes sense that those who are willing to start over again so readily in their jobs and careers must also have similar tendencies when it comes to love. (If you are interested in this particular topic, consider downloading the fascinating academic paper, <u>Till stress do us part: the causes and consequences of expatriate divorce</u>.

Thankfully I married someone who also has wanderlust and therefore we just wander together after some mutual consent on where and how we will wander. We think of it as being "unrealistic together." Sure, we have marital spats just like anyone else, but we are fortunate to have a healthy sense of what to keep and what to throw out in our lives. This can only work because of trust. There are no guarantees in life or love so you just have to choose wisely and do your best as you go along no matter what changes come.

So to succeed then at having a location-independent business, you must also be able to trust yourself, learn from your mistakes, and do your best as you go along no matter what changes come.

How can you build that trust and also protect yourself in the event that things don't go as planned? Here are my top tips for those embarking on the digital nomad journey:

- **Don't put all your eggs in one basket.**
  If you are making ecourses, don't just make a few lessons and sell them from one platform. If you offer consulting services, don't keep tapping into the same people to get work. If you freelance on *Fiverr.com*, start looking into a few more platforms as well as promoting yourself from your own website, etc. You get the idea right? Diversify, diversify, diversify!

I started in 2014 making online courses using the online learning platform *Udemy*. Along the way I expanded to also use *Skillfeed* (now defunct), *Skillshare*, *OfCourse*, *Curious.com*, *ViddyUp* (whom I later had to ditch) and others. Most recently I have set up my own online school from my own platform that I have much more control over.

I also started teaching online for the UN's University for Peace in Costa Rica and here in Myanmar I am affiliated with American University of Myanmar and teaching live courses for the creative professionals at Mango Group.

The point is, if one of my revenue sources dries up, which can happen quite easily especially in the digital realm, I have other income streams still available. I constantly assess and reassess what is working and what is not and adjust accordingly. I recommend you do the same. Start out simple of course, but slowly expand so all your eggs are not in one basket.

- **Never stop learning.**
  Unless you went to business school (and perhaps even if you did) there is still much to learn about the tools and platforms you will be using, not to mention that things are always changing. Then besides all the tech stuff (software, apps, equipment, etc.) there are things like creating quality content and the dreaded "m-word," marketing.

  We all excel at different things. For me, creating quality content came most naturally as well as mastering webcams, microphones, lighting, software, and all the rest. But I really was a know-nothing when it came to spreading the word, finding new online students and clients, promotions, and marketing.

  I actually now know what a lead magnet and marketing funnel are (even if I am still not sure what to do with them!) And I learned that "conversions" have nothing to do with religious fanaticism. (Unless the religion is marketing that is…)

  So bookmark useful-looking articles you come across online and save for later. Read books to help you get up to speed. Join *Facebook* and *LinkedIn* groups where other digital nomads hang out. Make friends with them and allow them to teach you what they know and you can do the same. Learn a little bit each day and then look back in awe after a few months to a year to see how far you've come.

- **Always have a contingency plan**
  In Myanmar the Internet is quite spotty so I try and work offline when the web is not available as well as upload large video files before going to bed in the hopes they will be ready in the morning.

  It seems like a major downer, but not really. After a few months of this it has become my new normal. I may however cry real tears of joy when I get access to a faster connection on our travels outside the country. (Seriously, I plan to open 15+ browser windows when we next visit Germany and then let them *all load at once*. Ah! That will hit the spot!)

  What is *your* contingency plan? What will you do if your computer fails or the power goes out? What if one of your revenue sources dries up overnight? Can you be flexible and make changes on the fly? Could you do some traditional or in-person work to help balance the scales? It's important to ask yourselves these kinds of questions before you even begin.

Kristen

So, potential budding digital nomad, you might also like to think of this journey metaphorically as if you were starting a garden. Which seeds will you sow today? How will you tend to your garden? Did the tomatoes (online *Udemy* courses) do better than the spinach (e-courses on your own self-hosted platform)? Plant more tomatoes while you work on improving your spinach crop! Maybe phase out spinach all together if things don't improve within a year and try radishes (freelance copywriting). Maybe see how some green beans (writing blog articles for companies) might do, etc. You get the idea right? And if not, go have some veggies and come back to me. They will help clear your head.

One last thing I will add here is that it can take a while to get started and see results where you are in a position to pay all your bills from only your online activities. If you have the ability to start as a digital nomad while doing other kinds of location-based work, preferably with a steady paycheck, I highly recommend you start when the stakes are low and landlords and collection agents are not breathing down your neck for overdue payments.

Good luck if you decide to go down this most exciting of paths and do send us a postcard from your adventures on the road. Cheers!

SOME FINAL KEY POINTS TO REMEMBER

- **Make a list of all the things you can potentially do as a digital nomad.** Then look at your list and choose one or two things you love and *want* to do and will actually try. Find others who are already successfully doing those things, join their conversations and glean their insights in the social media groups where they hang out, and get started taking those first baby steps towards following in their footsteps.

- **Don't put all your eggs in one basket.** Income streams come and go more quickly in the online realm so make sure to have a Plan B (and C, D, and E) to act as your safety net.

- **Failure is not a bad thing.** Failure is just feedback. Use what you learn to help you take that all-important next step.

- **You may be "loosey-goosey" with wherever it is you call home, but *do* remember to ensure that all your paperwork, taxes, visas, SIM cards, and everything else you need to keep your business running are in order.** It's OK to change your location with wherever the wind blows you, but do still stay as organized as you would if you had a location based office. You don't want to miss important payments or tax deadlines in your host or home countries. Stay in the loop and keep your new enterprise afloat wherever you may go.

OK. We have covered a lot of ground by this point. So what if you eventually decide that you've had your fill and are ready to take a stab at returning to your home country? Let's see what challenges and opportunities await you in the next chapter shall we?

Chapter 7: Maximizing Your Experience. Tips For Those Returning Home

> *"Maybe you had to leave in order to really miss a place; maybe you had to travel to figure out how beloved your starting point was."*
> — Jodi Picoult (Handle With Care)

How to Boost Your Career Back at Home With Your New International Experience

Kristen

Does international experience in your field set you apart once you return back home? I can only speak from my own experience, but I would say an enthusiastic yes!

We live in an increasingly global society and even if one were to never leave their own city of birth, chances are quite high that even firmly planted at home you will come across immigrants, foreigners, tourists, or even just fellow citizens who have been to other countries. Therefore, it is considered to be a great "21st century skill" to be able to communicate, work with, and relate to people from different cultures and life backgrounds.

In fact, organizations like **Ashoka** https://www.ashoka.org/ are making these "global citizenship skills" along with "empathy" and "change-making" top educational priorities for teaching young children moving forward in American schools in particular.

International businesses and organizations are increasingly working beyond their local communities where they are located physically and dealing with others at the international level, so the more you can interact with the global as well as local community, the better. And bonus points if you speak or are learning another language or two (or three...) All of these things should help give you an edge in most job interviews once you return home.

What do you think Jacqui?

Jacqueline

Unfortunately, I only had negative experiences on this score, and I'm unsure whether it was personal or whether my timing was wrong, but I found only disadvantages to returning to Australia after being abroad.

As I note in the next section, we returned to Australia in 2014 and planned an extended stay home. It was soon after a federal election that had seen a change in government, and the new conservative crew was making its presence felt in many aspects of life starting with the "welcome" from passport control at Sydney Airport.

"How long will you be staying?", the woman asked while examining my Australian passport.

"I'm coming home," I replied, jetlagged after over 40 hours on the road with my young son.

"But how long will you be staying?" she asked again, eyeing me suspiciously.

In my tired brain I wondered at this question – since when does an Australian citizen need to justify coming back into their own country? Can I not just come home? Clearly not.

"I'd like to stay as long as possible," I eventually replied, trying not to sound suspicious or annoyed. "I've been away in Germany for so long, I need to see the sun."

It wasn't a good answer, but for goodness sake… what else was I supposed to say? Passport control officers don't seem to share our footloose and fancy-free Wanderlust. I guess they don't get paid to.

And really, that welcome should have been an indication of what was to come. In eight months, the only work I was able to find was as an exam invigilator, earning temp wages.

Now, am I complaining? Heck yes! I hold an Honours degree, am a qualified corporate trainer, language trainer, and instructional designer. And despite the fact I've managed my own successful business in a foreign country, speak two languages, and am clearly adaptable and (if I do say so!) rather personable, there was absolutely no work to be found.

Being international was, in fact, a distinct disadvantage, even within the multicultural community of Canberra, Australia's capital. And why? Nobody knew me. Nobody could recommend me or speak to my experience. It was not possible to "translate" my ten years of success into a local context. Add to that the government's freeze on public service hires – and the ripple effect in the Canberra context on NGOs and the private sector – and you see that in an already tight job market, strangers were not welcome.

So does international experience boost your career opportunities at home? Yes, and no. It can, but it absolutely depends on the context. And this really is a warning, or at least a yellow flag. Think about what your work is, where you are, and what the market is like. Plan accordingly. Whereas some industries welcome international experience with open arms, others throw up their arms in despair because you don't fit inside their predefined boxes.

My mistake was assuming that Australia wanted me as much as I yearned for it. My advice to you is not to make the same mistake – plan ahead, be sensible, and be realistic.

REVERSE CULTURE SHOCK

Jacqueline

One thing I appreciate about living here in Germany is the German government's decision to welcome over one million asylum seekers. Now, that may make you a little upset or concerned – I know it's a hot political issue. But I am an optimist, and I focus on positives, on people, and on finding ways of walking together.

What does this have to do with reverse culture shock? Think about this: whereas Germany welcomed so many asylum seekers, both on a political and a personal level, the Australian government continues to demonise asylum seekers, keeping them in illegal offshore detention and perpetuating the myth of "queue jumpers," of the "dangerous foreigner." For a country with 220+ years of immigration, originally stolen from its initial inhabitants, it is a bit rich. But anyway...

So I travelled from Germany to Australia and was immediately struck by the anti-foreign sentiment, the "Australia: If you don't love it, leave" bumper stickers, and the Southern Cross "patriots."

That hurt a little.

Actually a lot.

The other aspect of reverse culture shock that really stung was on an environmental level – as I mentioned earlier, we Aussies are shocking when it comes to recycling. Absolutely shocking. Whereas in Germany almost everything can be and is recycled (there are even community compost schemes in some of the larger cities), it seemed to me that Aussies threw everything away. Plastic bottles on the street, for example. Ouch!

Small things like recycling and big things like asylum seeker policy were the shocks for me going back home to Australia.

When we focus on the topic of work, though, it struck me that the makeup of the workforce had changed. Or rather, it's that hiring practices had changed as well as hiring philosophies. For example, the capacity for international experience or a career path outside "the norm" to be understood and "translated" into a local context was missing. In my observation there were jobs which existed in boxes associated with clearly-defined norms, and deviation from these norms was an automatic rejection. Transferrable skills were not as important as direct experience. That's not at all what I expected, as I touched on earlier. This was jarring, not only professionally but also personally, and the question I asked myself again and again when I was back home in Australia was: how can one person be so successful in one country, and yet be invisible in the other?

Kristen, what about you? I think there was something we once spoke about concerning fresh food?

Kristen

OK. Yes, it's true that my time in Italy, one of the food capitals of the world, has spoiled me. While there is no shortage of things to stick in your pie-hole in the USA, it can take quite a bit of looking around that gigantic mega super-duper market to find foods not already laced with chemicals, pesticides, hormones, genetically modified organisms, preservatives, and additives. And once you *do* find the organic aisle, brace yourself for the major price increase!

I will say this though. Reverse culture shock can also be a great wake-up call. It can help you notice things about your own country and culture you'd perhaps like to tinker with and make even better thanks to your new insights.

For example, let's pretend for a moment that I was a chef and just came back to the USA after having lived in Italy and experienced the superiority of using fresh but simple high-quality ingredients in my cooking every time. Would that not then give me an edge over my American competitors firing up their microwaves and sharpening their can openers? Did I not just have real culinary experiences richer than what one may read about in a book?

Yes, perhaps I could have stayed home and just gone to the very expensive restaurant (with the two month waiting list) near my own hometown with the "authentic Roman chef." But wouldn't I learn more talking to real Italian farmers, olive growers, and little old ladies on a pensioner's budget making "peasant" bread soup, outdoor market grocers, *trattoria* owners, and regular everyday food-lovers in their own natural habitat in Italy?

The point is, your experiences abroad were a gift. Should you then be returning home, you now have an opportunity to share those gifts with everyone else.

Expat Tales: Brie -American Living in Germany

"I think the only difficulty I would have moving back to the States would be going through reverse culture shock. I notice so many cultural differences when I'm in the US, even just traveling there for a couple of weeks require some re-adjusting.

I lived very centrally in Bonn and Cologne, and now in Frankfurt. Life takes place on the streets. It takes only minutes to pop into the grocery store, the bank, and the pharmacy all on foot or by bike. In the suburbs in the US, you're completely dependent on a car."

RECONNECTING WITH YOUR HOME COUNTRY

Jacqueline

As I briefly mentioned earlier, when we returned to Australia for an extended stay in 2014 it was a complete culture shock. I love my country, but had it always been so ocker? So intolerant? So loud? Had food always been so expensive, bread so inedible, gardens so messy? And why were people confused by my accent, asking where I came from? Could they not hear that I'm an Aussie? Apparently not!

Living abroad for so long had changed much more than the way I lived and saw the world. It had changed the way the world heard me. I was a foreigner in my own land, and it took a long time to rebuild a connection.

So what I'm trying to say is that a reconnection with your home may take some time to establish. You may find yourself at odds with a culture you once accepted without question, you may find yourself questioning norms which once went unnoticed, and you may find yourself craving smells, sights, sounds, people, places, the light of the moon on a snowy garden, the sound of a brisk summer breeze whipping through the trees. Or even an East German pedestrian light: the man in the green hat.

Friends move on, too. Friends whom you crave when travelling, working and living abroad, friends who've lifted you up, shared unforgettable moments with – suddenly they can seem like near-strangers. If there's one thing I can prepare you for which is not work-related, it's this. Manage your expectations when you come home, and you find yourself sitting in a restaurant with two besties feeling like the third wheel, like you could walk out and they wouldn't even notice. Reintegration can take time, understanding, patience, and good humour. From experience I ask – keep yours!

Jacqueline's feet back on Australian shores. 2014.

FOREVER SMUG

Kristen

Not everyone working abroad eventually returns to their home country for good, but many do. They do so to be closer to family perhaps. It could be because of a health issue, to start anew once more, or just because of a desire to live somewhere more predictable again.

For those who have gone home again, while it may take a while to get all the reverse culture shock out of your system, one day you'll find that life is a tad easier than you remembered it.

You can understand (most of) what other people are saying because you are speaking the same language. You have a deep familiarity with a particular town, neighborhood, or street because it's where you grew up. You have a shared history and a connection that feels grounding rather than constraining like perhaps it once did.

Yes, the new and unexpected can be delightful, especially while off exploring foreign lands. But familiarity can also be delightful.

The place you may have returned to seems unchanged on the surface but somehow it is different and so are you. You are both *more* somehow. Your experiences have shaped you and through your experiences you will now shape your life back in your original home country.

And this time around you have new stories to share, lessons learned, and inspirations to try new things in old places. You might even be smug. Who wouldn't be?

So before you take the leap and set off on your own international adventure, let's now look to those who have already been there and ask if they think it was all worth it.

Chapter 8: Is It Worth It? Let Me Work It –Expat Reflections on the Good, the Bad, and the Ugly

"Life might be difficult for a while, but I would tough it out because living in a foreign country is one of those things that everyone should try at least once. My understanding was that it completed a person, sanding down the rough provincial edges and transforming you into a citizen of the world." — David Sedaris

Kristen

As we begin to slowly make our descent and bring this book in for a landing, we wanted to leave you with some final words of wisdom and advice from our fellow expatriate contributors.

We asked them what they wished they knew before starting their global adventures as well as what advice they might have for other budding explorers who are ready to take a flying leap into the great unknown.

From my end, I'm actually thankful that I *didn't* know in advance what I know now regarding my own personal experiences living abroad. For me, ignorance truly was bliss in the sense that had I known how hard some of the challenges would be beforehand, I probably never would have taken the leap.

If my husband Michael and I had known for example back in 2006 that Rome really was not like most other big international cities (such as London, Paris, New York, Berlin, etc.) and that it would take so long and be so difficult for Michael to find work in finance there, I might never have signed my contract at The American University of Rome and quit my already great tenure-track job at William Paterson University in Wayne, New Jersey.

More simply put, because we didn't know that "two foreigners with limited Italian and zero connections getting good jobs in Rome was impossible," as a result it *was* possible. It was possible because we both believed we could make a good life there and as a result serendipity and opportunities presented themselves, albeit in their own time frame, not ours.

So my best advice for those still on the fence about making a go of it working abroad is be as prepared as possible. Do your research, get your paperwork in order, start your language lessons way before you arrive, begin making friends and connections online, update and hone your skills, and polish up that resume.

Arrive in your new country as a beacon of light just waiting to share your unique skills and talents. But also expect difficulties and setbacks, Expect to be blown off course completely at times and to feel like a damn fool. Play chicken with your own fear of failure and win. Or lose and pick yourself back up again as a reinvented version of yourself.

Come with an open mind and optimistic attitude. And now's a *great* time to take up visualization (or manifestation, or positive affirmations, etc.) They really *do* make a difference in helping you design your own life! I read Shakti Gawain's groundbreaking book, *Creative Visualization* when I was twenty and my life hasn't been the same since. (In a good way.)

Transform your fears that the world is unsafe into a knowing that everything is going to be OK and life and circumstances *will* take care of you. Then get on that airplane, train, bus, boat, or spacecraft and zoom towards your own unique destiny.

Now over to Jacqueline for her take on things…

Jacqueline

Thanks, Kristen!

This whole book, the writing process, has given me pause for thought and reflection. See, moving abroad for me wasn't a huge conceptual leap, as that's how we grew up. My parents took us four children across the globe, and my childhood memories are redolent of the aromas of Chandigarh, the heat of the Taj Mahal in Agra under my 4-year-old feet. School in PNG and having a *puk-puk* (crocodile) in the back garden is a normal seven-year-old memory for me, as is crossing the Samoan island of Upolu as a 12-year-old to spend a Sunday afternoon on Tafatafa beach, or walking around Lake Geneva in the snow.

As a child, we would always leave home and we would always return. As a child, the leaving was difficult – farewelling friends and the security of home, but the coming home was also difficult. I cried when we left Samoa and my cat Ginger had to be left behind.

We would come back to Australia and things would be the same and yet different – friends would have moved on, fashions would have changed and we would have been left behind, TV shows would have come and gone and we'd never have heard of them, not be able to participate in conversations about favourite characters or storylines.

But these are the impressions and memories of a child. And though it may sound dire, parents don't let it dissuade you! I'd never for a moment change my childhood! Children are resilient.

Kristen mentioned that she's so glad that she and Michael didn't know all the ups and downs, ins and outs in advance. To a certain extent, neither did I when I started this voyage. I came to Germany expecting another short trip before a return home to Australia. And here I am, almost 11 years on, married, mum, business owner. Completely unplanned.

So, I'm not going to say something pithy like: *Hey! Congratulations! Now you're a global citizen!* Because I know how hard it can be on the heart and head when you're finding your feet again. But remember – it was worth it, all the travel, the work abroad, the friends you made, the experiences you had. Everything has been worth it. You are enriched by it.

But that's my perspective. Here are some insights from some of our contributors on the topic:

More Tips From Our Fellow Expats

Heather LaBonte Efthymiou -American Living in Cyprus, Formerly in the UK

"I can't say that it was all bad; my living in Europe. I did meet many interesting people from all walks of life. I also got to see how people in other countries viewed my country. I feel everyone should get to see this as it can help relations between countries if we understand each other better.

I was, for the most part, happy with the Universal Health Care system in the UK. It made me very interested in voting for such a thing in the USA. In Cyprus, I have been appreciative of the low violent crime rate. It is nice to not have to look over your shoulder at night in case there is a rapist or mugger. I've also learned to be grateful for many of the prices of things we have in the USA like gasoline (petrol). Americans do complain a lot about gas prices but many are completely unaware of how cheap they get their gas compared to many other countries in the world.

Being away from my country for so many years I came to appreciate many things I took for granted."

Sweety -Indian Living in the USA

"Working in the USA has been so encouraging and inspiring. Every time I do something, I find some new way to develop and be more successful. As they say, America is the land of opportunity. I truly believe it is and it makes you keep on going. You definitely get rewarded for all the hard work that you do."

Valerie Chaboud -Brazilian who lived in the USA, Australia, Switzerland, and France

"Things changed in my life and I eventually decided to go back to Brazil. I miss a lot my life in Europe, but now is a new stage in my life where in my own home country I can´t get a job.

So, if you have a chance to go overseas, just go and enrich your life experience even if sometimes they are not so good because this experience you will take with you for the rest of your life. Good luck!"

Justin P. Moore -American Living in Germany

"Getting settled and finding my groove working abroad took time, patience, and persistence.

There are certainly many factors to making it work-- some controllable, many circumstantial. Learning the local language and adapting to the culture differences were crucial to my success, and in my mind essential for a long-term strategy.

Many countries and locations work well for short-term plans and projects, but I have always recommended learning at least the functional basics of the local language-- out of respect and to really open the doors of possibility.

It took me almost six months of intense study of German to become confident and conversational, and another few months to really feel expressive and more natural.

I also advocate full immersion and trying to speak, read, write, and work in the local language from the start. For me, this meant getting a German roommate, an internship at a gallery, and spending as much time as possible with locals.

It took me several years to understand the differences in the work world-- particularly business partner and client relationship differences as a designer and artist. German working relationships take months and years of trust building to become solid, and it took me a long time to realize that Germans do not take as many risks or value

*innovation as much as refinement and doing things
more slowly, traditionally, and safely.*

*It also took me years to find the proper balance of
my unique personal and professional perspectives
and approach to creativity against doing things in
ways that were more familiar to my clients and
partners."*

Kristen

We could happily go on with the advice and
encouragement from our expatriate friends around the
world. Instead let's end this chapter with a short and
snappy quote that particularly resonates with me and
hopefully will inspire you to take action (now or
sometime in the future when the time is right).

> "A ship is safe in harbor, but that's not what
> ships are for." *–William G.T. Shedd*

Kristen teaching in Yangon, Myanmar at Mango Group. 2017.

CONCLUSION

"May the road rise up to meet you. May the
wind always be at your back. May the sun
shine warm upon your face, and rains fall soft
upon your fields and until we meet again,
may God hold you in the palm of His hand."
— Traditional Gaelic Blessing

TIME TO WRITE YOUR OWN STORY

Jacqueline

Thank you for coming on this journey with us through
the ins and outs, ups and downs of working abroad.
It's exciting, rewarding, challenging, scary and
unforgettable. Approaching it with open eyes and a
well-laid plan is essential, but that shouldn't take away
from the beauty of spontaneity and call of adventure.

We hope we've filled your cup full of ideas, we've
inspired you to take that step abroad, and we've
equipped you with useful tips, tricks, and resources to
get you going. And we hope to hear from you with
your experiences, feedback, and questions.

Best of luck for your journey ahead, and may the road
truly rise to meet you!

Kristen

Thanks Jacqui! I too hope that the experiences, insights, and resources in this book have given you more strength and resolve to go on your own overseas work and volunteer adventures.

So we bid you a smug goodbye (or maybe just a smug "see you later") and hope that we've given you much to ponder. If we really succeeded, you are already full of ideas and are itching to get started putting your plans into action.

Please note, we have a growing list of our very favorite and most essential travel and working abroad resources including how to get the cheapest airfares, best hotel deals, and more. Get your free 6-page PDF guide by signing up for our bi-monthly Free At Last Newsletter full of travel advice, inspirations, deals, and more. You can also find us at http://liveloveworkabroad.com .

Finally, don't forget to come join us in our Facebook Group, Free At Last: Live, Love & Work Abroad to share your own stories, ask Jacqueline and myself for specific travel or working abroad advice, and to meet other readers embarking on a similar international journey. See you there!

Acknowledgements

KRISTEN

Thanks first and foremost to my co-author Jacqueline. She has an infectious, playful spirit and has been fabulous to work with. Thanks also to our wonderful editors Gidget Harris and Deborah Wojcicki, all our international contributors who generously shared their stories, and our dedicated beta-readers who gave us early feedback on the book.

Of course, it goes without saying that I am grateful to my supportive husband Michael and my gorgeous sons Lukas and Nico for being my biggest cheerleaders as well as my family and friends in Swansea, Massachusetts. You are loved and appreciated more than you know.

Finally, a special thank you goes to all my wonderful, secret writing spots: somewhere by the turtle pond in *Villa Sciara* in Rome, Italy, Jacqueline's cozy living room in Rentzschmühle, Germany, and a hodge-podge assortment of lovely parks, lakes, and coffee shops in Yangon, Myanmar.

JACQUELINE

My thanks go to my brilliant co-author Kristen, who's

an inspiration as well as a great friend, and the champion of butt-kickers when my writing fell by the wayside. Thanks!

My husband Ralf, our son and sunshine James, my "big German brother" Michael, and those who brought down The Wall get a huge thanks from me – without all of them, my German story wouldn't exist.

And finally, thanks to my parents Chris and Dianne, who infused me with the travel bug, who took us to India, Papua New Guinea, Samoa, the wrong train across Europe, and a dodgy café in Brindisi... We are the road less travelled.

About The Authors

Kristen Palana

Kristen Palana is an artist, educator, and author currently living and working in Yangon, Myanmar.

Since 2000 she has taught undergraduate and graduate university students in Rome, Italy as well as in and around the NYC area, USA. Kristen is also part of the extended team at the UN-mandated *University For Peace* in Costa Rica where she teaches online for their *Centre For Executive Education*. Since 2014 Kristen also teaches 30K+ online students from over 165 countries.

Kristen is a dual American/Portuguese citizen and has presented art and multimedia courses in Africa, Asia, Europe, and North America. Her work is exhibited internationally and has received a number of awards.

Traveling and volunteering in developing countries rank among her biggest interests. She lives with her German husband Michael, Roman sons Lukas and Nico, and New Yorker cat Oliver.

Find out more at amazon.com/author/kristenpalana

Or visit (https://kpalana.com)

Jacqueline Seidel

Jacqueline Seidel is an Australian business skills and language trainer who has been based in Germany since early 2006. Her professional background is originally in the Australian private and public sectors, and she combines this business and policy background with a passion for providing interesting, engaging, and enjoyable training programs.

Through her company, O'Connell Advanced Training Solutions, she provides advanced coaching and development in more effective business English communication, delivered through competency-based, customised, individual, or small group training programs.

As a child, she grew up in India, Papua New Guinea, Western Samoa, and had a small stint in Switzerland where she developed a love of Toblerone and an aversion to snow!

Find out more at: http://www.amazon.com/-/e/B01CCY12GC

Or visit: www.oconnell-training.com

Other Books By Kristen Palana and Jacqueline Seidel

Free At Last: Live, Love and Work Abroad as a 21st Century Global Citizen

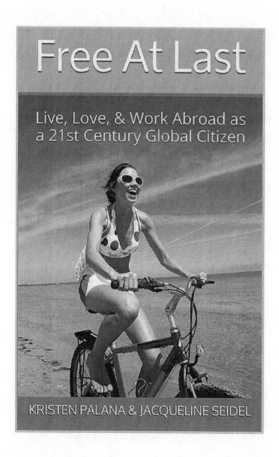

Are you ready to go global? Whether you are firmly planted in your familiar hometown or are already making plans for your exotic wedding in India next December, this book will help you connect with this great and wonderful world that we share with 7 billion+ others in your own way, in your own time, and at your own pace.

Part travel guide and part memoir, this book gets into the inner world and psychology of becoming a traveler and expatriate, providing insights on the ups, downs, obstacles, and epiphanies of life both on and off the road.

Full of true stories, inspirations, hard-won advice, and sneaky tricks, this guide will help you bring the world to your own doorstep when you can't get away, inspire you to take your first trip outside your hometown, and get you started studying, volunteering, and working abroad on the right foot. Then, if you really get into the thick of things, you might find yourself actually falling in love, getting married, and even giving birth abroad. What then? Been there. Done that.

Authors Kristen Palana and Jacqueline Seidel are female travelers and expatriates with decades of experience living, studying, backpacking, volunteering, working, and parenting abroad. Get their perspective when you no longer know what to say when people ask you where you are from and worlds start colliding!

Welcome to the world of becoming more worldly.
Let's get you started on your own unique journey!

Find this book at Amazon or by visiting **kpalana.com.**

Crowdfunding Confidential: Raise Money For You and Your Cause

Crowdfunding Confidential is a friendly, funny, clear, and EFFECTIVE guide to successfully planning, crafting, and launching a crowdfunding campaign that meets its goal for you or someone in need. **Who will you help today and what are you waiting for?**

Grab this quick yet powerful guide and get your successful crowdfunding campaign off on the right foot so you can help others in need starting today. This easy to follow handbook, written to be conversational and accessible will empower YOU to plan, create, and manage your first successful online crowdfunding campaign even if you have no previous fundraising experience and no idea where to start.

Busy working mother, college professor, and serial crowdfunder Kristen Palana, has raised over $125K online for 90+ housing, health, education, and income generation projects for needy children and their families since 2004 in her so-called spare time. This book delivers eleven years-worth of her best hard-won advice and tips for successful online crowdfunding so that you can get started helping others in need powerfully and effectively right away.

This book is a companion to Kristen Palana's online course by the same name.

Find this book at Amazon or by visiting **kpalana.com.**

Teaching English – Your Guide To Launching Your Successful ESL Teaching Career

Taking your first solo steps as an ESL trainer can be daunting – Jacqueline Seidel knows. She's been there! But for the past ten years Seidel has developed a strong, successful business where demand has always exceeded capacity, where clients have consistently re-signed, and where she has reaped the rewards of professionalism, creativity, flexibility and drive.

In this eBook, which complements a Udemy course of the same name, Seidel offers you her framework for success in easy-to-follow, bite-sized steps demonstrated with real-life examples and activities you can do to focus your business ideas and personal branding.

A career in ESL training is professionally and personally rewarding, and Jacqueline Seidel's pleasure to walk with you on your path to success.

Find this book at Amazon or by visiting **oconnell-training.com.**

MAY WE PLEASE ASK A FAVOR?

If there's someone you know who could benefit from this book, please DO let them know by spreading the word.

Also, you can help this book have a larger impact and reach simply by leaving a quick (or slow) review on Amazon once you are finished with it. We read every review personally and would be extremely grateful for your feedback. The more reviews this book gets, the more visibility it will have and the more other people can know if it might be a helpful resource for them.

If you'd like to leave a review then please visit our book at Amazon.com.

Review Free At Last: Live, Love, and Work Abroad. Find Jobs and Build Your Career From Anywhere

Thanks for your support!

Made in the USA
San Bernardino, CA
20 December 2017